Achieving Differentiated Learning

Achieving Differentiated Learning

Using the Interactive Method Workbook

Marjorie S. Schiering

ROWMAN & LITTLEFIELD
Lanham • Boulder • New York • London

Published by Rowman & Littlefield
An imprint of The Rowman & Littlefield Publishing Group, Inc.
4501 Forbes Boulevard, Suite 200, Lanham, Maryland 20706
www.rowman.com

6 Tinworth Street, London, SE11 5AL, United Kingdom

Copyright © 2019 by Marjorie S. Schiering

All figures created by the author.

All rights reserved. No part of this book may be reproduced in any form or by any electronic or mechanical means, including information storage and retrieval systems, without written permission from the publisher, except by a reviewer who may quote passages in a review.

British Library Cataloguing in Publication Information Available

Library of Congress Cataloging-in-Publication Data

Names: Schiering, Marjorie S., 1943– author.
Title: Achieving differentiated learning : using the interactive method workbook / Marjorie S. Schiering.
Description: Lanham : Rowman & Littlefield, [2019] | Includes bibliographical references. |
Identifiers: LCCN 2019010819 (print) | LCCN 2019019534 (ebook) | ISBN 9781475831757 (Electronic) | ISBN 9781475831733 (cloth : alk. paper) | ISBN 9781475831740 (pbk. : alk. paper)
Subjects: LCSH: Individualized instruction. | Children with disabilities—Education. | Student-centered learning. | Teaching—Methodology.
Classification: LCC LB1031 (ebook) | LCC LB1031 .S26 2019 (print) | DDC 371.39/4—dc23
LC record available at https://lccn.loc.gov/2019010819

Contents

Foreword	vii
Preface	ix
Prelude	xi
Acknowledgments	xiii
Introduction	xv

PART I: EXPLAINING THE INTERACTIVE METHOD (IM) REGARDING THINKING SKILLS, MEMORY, AND CLASSROOM IMPLEMENTATION

1	Explaining the Interactive Method (IM): Experience-Based Teaching and Learning	3
2	Reciprocal Thinking, Cognitive Collective, and Memories: The Teaching of Thinking	9
3	Addressing Different Ways Through Assignments, Requirements, and Purposes	19

PART II: DIFFERENT LEARNERS = DIFFERENT WAYS: THE "HOW TO" OF THE IM

4	Different Ways: Six Specific Types	29
5	Twenty-Five Different Ways	33
6	Twenty-Eight Different Ways	51
7	Different Ways with 13 Examples: Technology	69
8	Activity-Based Learning Center (ABLC): Trifold Boards	77
9	Graphic Organizers/Text Structures and Four Interactive Instructional Resources: Directions and Application	79

PART III: PERSONAL COMMENTARIES ON SPECIAL NEEDS AND DIFFERENT ABILITIES AND CLOSING THOUGHTS

10	Personal Perspectives Regarding Parenting and/or Teaching Different Abilities and Special Needs Students	91
	Perspectives on a Learner's Dyslexia *Patricia Eckardt*	91
	From the Heart: Having Different Abilities Children: Their Dad's Narrative *Timothy Ryley*	95
	Commentary: Teaching Special Education Technology *Clare King*	97
11	Author's Closing Thoughts	99
	References	101
	About the Author	107

Foreword

Some years ago, Dr. Marjorie Schiering answered an ad for a teaching position at the University of Edinburgh, Scotland. When the interviewer asked her if she was a lecturer, meaning one who stood before her students and related her reflections on whatever subject, her response was no. A firm negative. Lecturing was not the way she learned to teach most effectively, and she had no desire to change. Her chosen approach to conveying ideas and information involved working with her students, instructing them by doing rather than having them listen. Well, she did not get the job but remained true to herself, to what she knew worked well.

In a series of books, *Achieving Differentiated Learning* being the most recent, Dr. Schiering shares with educators and teacher candidates a method she has used and perfected over decades of successful classrooms. She offers scholarly support for her method, which she traces back 100 years, but also offers her unique twists on the concept and solid evidence of its value. Replete with illustrations of how she translates the theory of interactive education to practical applications, the book offers her experience to all who face a gathering of students not always eager to engage in or prepared for the work of learning.

In the present environment, where young people are less inclined to read or to sit still for a spoken lesson than were students of earlier generations, the hands-on, interactive, experiential, or multimodal approach Dr. Schiering develops in this text can be especially effective in reaching these current learners.

What comes through when one reads Dr. Schiering's books is something more than conveyed information. Most evident is her respect for and desire to help all students, especially those facing physical, social, or mental difficulties, those identified as having "different abilities." She loves her students, each and every one of them. She loves teaching. We who work with her and witness her energy, creativity, and wisdom attest to her success in her classes. She seeks to share this love and care with all who aspire to work with the young and to encourage her peers to neglect not one student before them. Careful study of what this book contains will help the teacher and the student learn—and learn well.

Robert Kinpoitner, PhD
Chairman of the Royal English Department
Molloy College
Rockville Centre, NY

Preface

Perhaps you should first know that this book and its companion one are written in the fashion of having a conversation with you, the reader. You are asked questions in hopes you'll reflect on them and share your thoughts and feelings with others. Having related that, you are invited to examine the content of this second book in this two-book series. In this "companion" book, there's the addressing of different ways of teaching and learning for different abilities students, and that includes those who may have special needs. *These are defined as learners' instruction requiring application of a nontraditional instructional methodology, as traditional methodologies don't necessarily accommodate all students with "different abilities."*

For the writing on these pages, types of disorders are considered to be part of "different abilities," as each one will impact an individual's learning. What the Interactive Method (IM) proposes in both books is that the interaction of learning—the "doing"—results in student involvement and engagement, which leads to retention of information/material. In a manner of speaking, the IM is a means of teaching thinking with the use of the Reciprocal Thinking Phases: Cognition and Metacognition (see Chapter 2).

As you read the pages and as you peruse the content, take time to analyze the principles in these 11 chapters. Then, consider at some point "selecting" activities to actually implement in your classroom or in your daily teaching and learning practices. For what, you may question? The answer would be for the betterment of learning in general.

Primarily, this second book provides "different ways" of teaching and learning by having experiences in which students are involved, through a multimodality approach, to material that's part of a curriculum—the curriculum that is at any grade level. Sometimes educational jargon refers to "different ways" as "experiential" learning and other times as "hands-on" instruction or "differentiated learning." This author refers to different ways as implementing instruction through practicing the Interactive Method. That is the term used in this two-book series. Whichever term is used, the idea is that there is "interactive" teaching and learning that "engages" the students in being personally "involved" in their acquisition and retention of curriculum.

Dewey called this *engagement-in-learning, Experientialism*, in the 1930s. Today it's referred to as *Constructivism*. The idea is the same, however, in that information is disseminated through active engagement that has been put together in a practical manner that allows for guides, modeling, creativity, and critical thinking, simultaneously and reciprocally. And, with respect to different ways applying to special needs persons . . . well, reflectively speaking, at some juncture, we all may have special needs of one sort or another.

Have you ever heard the expression "There's nothing new in education"? The *New York Times* recently had an article by Valerie Strauss on December 12, 2018. The headline referred to this book's interactive content as being a "new rage in education." And this bold statement was followed with "never mind that it's a century old." Is nothing new in education? Perhaps that's true, nothing is new, as seen with the above comment about today's teaching practices being 100 years old; the previous reference to Dewey and the decades-old Dale's *Cone of Experience* (1946) theory would substantiate that.

With 90% of retention being achieved by what we both say and do, using a majority of our senses, the following might serve as examples of this experiential learning: storytelling, a dramatic presentation, simulating the real experience, and doing the real thing, such as making something like a diorama of a colonial settlement or a wall map of the planets in our solar system.

These previous paragraphs addressed learning in the first half of the 20th century and now you're invited to look back to the early 1700s in the United States. There were programs outside of school called *apprenticeships*.

Aside from the political ramifications or the original impact of indentured servitude, there were over 33 "trades" that had apprenticeship programs that later became, in some states, courses in school for tradesmen. Nonetheless, as explained by Jacoby in 1991, the instructional techniques for carpentry, coopering, sewing, printing, and the like were accomplished by tradesmen showing the trainee how things were to be done and the apprentice copying or "learning by doing."

Later, in many schools this came to be known as serving an internship as a teacher or administrator after courses had been taken to learn how to teach. This was replaced with college degrees in education, passing educational discipline-specific or multisubject comprehensive examinations that were given by the state. And then there was becoming a teacher to "practice" this craft.

This author states: "You're asked to look around you if you're in a classroom and if not, think of at least a few people you know. Recall what they generally wear, their facial features and physical appearance or mannerisms. In this reflection, do they look the same? Probably not. So, imagine this concept: if we don't look the same, we well may not learn the same way." Madeline Hunter (1964) exemplified this idea when she stated, "Expecting all children the same age to learn from the same material is like expecting all children the same age to wear the same size clothing."

Subsequently, as we each are dissimilar in appearance, so too are the instructional (academic) abilities and needs regarding learning. Along with that are the varieties of *social cognition* experienced. These are such things as room design; talking with others; being provided with comfort zones; chances to work alone or in partnerships, groups, and teams; and adherence to the idea of emotional safety in the classroom, with there being positivity instead of negativity. A learning environment where "lift-up" statements are predominant creates a sense of acceptance and approval. Each of these things, and many more, influences each individual's learning.

Not every activity is for every student, but modifications may be made to accommodate different abilities by using one's own imagination and ideas for alteration or adaptation. Basically, the ideas put forth on the following pages are designed to create interest, engage the student learners through experience, and provide for critical thinking being applied to creativity. The chapters' activities have instructional lessons that involve a multimodality approach. *Overall, this book acknowledges that we may not be the same, but we can learn the same material that's part of the curriculum.*

So while the method of instruction is very important, as the focal point of these two companion books, with examples for meeting the needs of student learners' developing their thinking skills, so too is the concept that we are always learning. And "we are all teachers of something" (Schiering, 2000–present, 2018). That "something" is what we model through our character and examples of learning techniques for varied learners' achieving *success* in the classroom setting. That last component leads to accomplishments and self-confidence in one's own interactions with others in and outside of the academic setting.

Achieving Differentiated Learning and the first book in this series, are based on concepts realized by this author's decades of teaching experience. This has been done with the idea of experiential learning whereby students are thoroughly engaged in their taking-in and retention of information yielding the best results regarding student academic and social success. This book has 3 parts and 11 chapters.

Prelude

Question: What is the purpose of using different ways, differentiation of instruction, differentiated learning strategies, or the Interactive Method (IM)/Experientialism when it comes to applying instructional techniques?

Answers:

1. Have different ways of instruction on which one can rely for the purpose of recalling material and practicing reflection.
2. Realize that the way one learns is acceptable, and learning through "doing" or being involved in the instructional method has been proven to provide "maximum retention of information" (Maheshwari addressing Dale's *Cone of Experience*, 2016).
3. Prepare the individual for doing well on tests or exams by teaching thinking.
4. Have means that can be continually utilized for creating memories, at home if not in the school.
5. Offer an entry-level means of instruction for developing a sense of self-confidence, efficacy, reliance, and the skills necessary for future learning challenges.
6. Transition from the "different ways" by embracing one's own ability to learn when it's job time, as opposed to schooling time.
7. Have personal learning techniques to rely on, at any stage of one's life, learning with comfort.

Acknowledgments

This book and its companion are about special needs, different abilities, and different ways to teach as well as learn. For the last of these, I have realized that no book gets written without assistance from a multitude of people. The ones at home probably come first. After that, there are those who contributed through their writing, those who didn't but encouraged, or those who are in each of these categories.

Then there's not just assistance for this book but for the ones that came before it, and those persons, if mentioned in this acknowledgments section, would possibly make it longer than this book itself. The reason for this is that one event leads to another, perhaps not right away, but at some point there is a connection. There's a bringing together of the people in our lives who were part of events to which there was a reaction, which led to another event and another reaction . . . until . . . the book gets written. At this juncture, I thank the following:

I give sincere appreciation to my husband, George. He literally devoted himself to my remaining on task and did a myriad of other things. Some of these include taking photos and configuring about 100 figures for this book, and a few for the first in this two-book series; making photocopies of needed material; conducting research pertinent to the topic of both books; sharing about my conference presentations and what was most effective, as well as proofreading the drafts of the first and second books and putting together the reference section of both manuscripts.

As if this were not enough, he created the website www.creativecognition4U.com, where one can go to see videos, which he recorded, of how to make the interactive instructional resources and see lesson photographs of teachers using "different ways" with the Interactive Method (IM).

In a previous paragraph, I mentioned how one event leads to another. Such is the case with the chairman of the Royal English Department (RED) at Molloy College, Robert Kinpoitner, PhD. Bob is acknowledged for his helpfulness, being a person who gives without asking for anything in return. He arranged for me to teach a children's literature course for the RED and he was also my grammarian on all of the books I've authored. He is additionally recognized for his impeccable sense of humor and continually being a person who lifts one's spirits with his positivity.

Angela Sullivan, a contributor to the first book's Chapter 2, is recognized for her "being present!" Her organizational skills provided assistance. But, most importantly, her friendship has been steadfast since we wrote together during our doctoral candidate years, 20 years ago. Once a teacher, then a school administrator, and at present a part-time professor, she continually practices and supports the ideas of the IM.

Drew Bogner, PhD, president of Molloy College, is mentioned for his coauthorship of *Teaching and Learning: A Model for Academic and Social Cognition* and most significantly for providing techniques addressing the "voice" of a book. His encouragement in the early 2000s served as the beginning "push" to start my writing endeavors at our institution.

Those who contributed to this book are given acknowledgment of the highest caliber. This is for taking time to write and share their expertise with respect to teaching that involves the IM and/or life experiences with a special needs or different abilities person(s).

Aside from those previously mentioned, contributors to this book or the first one in this series include Drs. Madeline Craig and Trish Eckardt; Pat Mason; and Professors Rickey Moroney, Maggie Blair, Marie Calder, and Tim Ryley. Next, there's Kevin Cooney, who is the Kiwanis Club advisor to Molloy's Circle K; Marc Hoberman; Clare King, a former teacher candidate and present special education technology teacher; Diana Abourafeh from the Rebecca Center for Music Therapy at Molloy; and Matthew and Jolie Schiering. These two of our six children wrote, respectively, for the first book about the effect of interactive instructional techniques on leadership building and thoughts on being a resource room special education teacher.

Eileen Chapman is acknowledged with gratitude for transcribing figures into PDFs and for her formatting endeavors for the first book, as well as for portions of this companion one. Additionally, Eileen did this for the book *What's Right With You: An Interactive Character Development Guide*. Eileen is a former colleague who became a friend and has been steadfast in assisting me with the technological components of writing.

This book has contributions from over 100 of Molloy's former or present teacher candidates. They are acknowledged here because of the work they have done to support and infuse interactive learning. These individuals took the time to use the IM in their classrooms or during student teaching. They applied instructional techniques that used activity-based learning and/or project-performance-based (P/PBL) instruction to pass along to others who teach special needs and different abilities students.

Tom Koerner, PhD, is a person whom happenstance presented to me. His publishing acumen, insight, and encouragement are unequaled. Once seeing a few Interactive Book Report samples, he heartened me to write about this activity-based strategy. That resulted in the 2016 workbook publication of *Teaching Creative and Critical Thinking: An Interactive Workbook*, as well as books before and after that. This included one on character development. He has been most instrumental in all of my publishing endeavors through offering advice and support. His associate, Carlie Wall, has continually been helpful with furthering my writing endeavors. For me, their assistance qualifies them as exceptional people.

There are others along the path of having one's book(s) published whose work is of utmost importance. These are the production editors and copyeditors. These individuals cross check what needs to be addressed in the manuscripts for clarification of thoughts or references and a myriad of other things. This occurs before the manuscript goes to typesetting. Respectively for the first and second books there are production editors Megan DeLancey and Lara Hahn and copyeditors Meghann French and Julia Loy who I thank for being mindful.

Again, as one thing is connected to another, there is appreciation for my 10th-grade social studies teacher, Ms. Carragher, who said, "I believe in you," which resulted in my thinking if she can do that, then perhaps I might believe in myself as well. Next, as one's experimental past affects the present and future, the following are acknowledged for the idea of assisting others along life's paths.

There are my parents, Mollie and Red After; my friend Daisy Schneider; and Rita Dunn, who served as my mentor in the St. John's University Instructional Leadership Doctoral Program. Her guidance brought me to presenting at schools here and abroad, as well as writing chapters in books. Her encouragement lives on with me to this day.

Last, but not least, are our children and their significant others: Matthew and Maddy, Alyssha and Paul Miro, Josh and Katie, Jolie, Mara and Dave Moore, and Seth and Carolina. Of course, our grandchildren, Jared, Rayna, Jacob, Bailey, Marina, Landyn, Eva, Eliana, Sam, Jonas, Levi, and Jewel, are appreciated for keeping me involved in what's "in" right now.

Introduction

Just the title of this book tells you, the reader, that it's about a style of teaching and learning. This is referred to as the Interactive Method (IM), and it serves as the core of emphasizing lessons that (1) involve, (2) engage, and (3) examine the "doing" part of education, where the learners partake in experientialism, as well as thinking about what one is thinking. For this book, such is described as being in the moment with critical thinking, designing, creating, and producing an end product, oftentimes for a presentation or performance.

The idea for such a book came from the concept of how you teach children with different abilities the same curriculum as children who are advanced in abilities or, at the opposite end of the spectrum, those who have special needs. In this second of the two-book series' beginning part, there's a brief iteration of differentiating between different abilities and special needs. The concept of Dr. Rita Dunn's 1970s statement "If children don't learn the way we teach, then we must teach them the way they learn" (1990, 15–18) is a mainstay for this entire book, and herein resides the concept of differentiated instructional practices. The book you're about to read has 50 years of collected teaching methods rolled into one . . . the IM.

The first three chapters address the ideas revolving around flexibility of thinking for all types of students. Oftentimes education itself gets into a "functional fixedness" (Mlodinow 2018/ 2019) where instructional thinking is the same for everyone. Such thinking and subsequent teaching and learning is patterned with ways to do things that have been experienced for, possibly, decades. There is no change . . . doing things the same way day after day, month after month, year after year is what's practiced. This can be referred to as being cognitively trapped.

This book you're holding calls attention to looking at what's to be taught through a "beginner's mind." Such a thinking style emphasizes a fresh start, "the beginner is empty, free of the habits of the expert, ready to accept, to doubt, and open to all the possibilities" (Suzuki, 1970). With that idea in mind, there's an explanation of a relatively new concept that refers to thinking as being a reciprocal process.

While thinking is indeed noted to have varied levels of complexity, this author postulates from her 20-plus years of research on this topic that one moves within and between these "levels" simultaneously from prelanguage through till much, much, much later years. This is whether one is in school or not. The thinking we do may be identified as to which skills are being realized at any given time. This identification allows for recognition (initial stage of thinking), comparing and contrasting (initial stage of thinking), prioritizing, deciding, and critical and creative thinking (intermediate stage) for evaluation and analysis with problem-solving (metacognitive stage/ highest order of thinking). A Reciprocal Thinking Chart is provided in Chapter 2 along with a Chart of Activities and an illustration of Applied Thinking Skills.

The highest of the highest level of thinking is self-actualizing, as one is taking action and "doing" something . . . having the experience with a product or performance as the immediate end result. In that vein, the IM is continually at the highest level of thinking while involving the other levels to achieve this goal. The Reciprocal Thinking Phases are shown to illustrate this hierarchy and reciprocal thinking process. Each of the experiences with thinking involve creating "memories" through interaction with the topic being addressed.

The first part of this book concludes with a college class's (EDU 5060) curriculum that is project and/or performance based. Simultaneously, the course assignments, inside and outside class discussions and practices, provide for the IM that may be used in these future teachers' classrooms. *This is regardless of whether the new teacher is in a mainstreamed classroom, a special education one, or a teacher of students of other languages. The IM may be used by all ability levels and any grade level.*

The remainder of this book has five chapters with narratives and illustrations of different activities. These are from a present or former teacher candidate, present or retired teacher, student learner, professor, or administrator. The source is important, but just as important is the activity, which is designed for optimum learning. In that vein, the Interactive Book Report (play the page) pages, Activity-Based Learning Centers, and Project- and/or Performance-Based Learning ideas are presented.

Uniquely, this book closes with commentaries or perspectives about being, teaching, or having children with different abilities and/or special needs. Ideas on how "different ways" worked as a means of educating them appear in the narratives. The author closes the chapters of this book with her own perspective on what's important in teaching regarding the social and academic parts of teaching and learning. A few thoughts are put forth and these are to not put yourself or others down but to provide lift ups and positivity, as the former serves no real purpose. Then there is the idea of one's being enough as is.

BOOK'S AUDIENCE

This book's for you! Who "you" are is a learner and teacher, as these titles are used interchangeably. As one learns, one teaches, and vice versa. This book is for those who want to engage the student learner in viable instructional situations that are enjoyable because of one's personal involvement. It's for those who love to discover and find wonderment in learning by using different means of instruction suited to their own interests or to student-learners' securities, methods, pace, ability level, perceptual preferences, processing styles, creative elements, tier lessons, and/or varied types of assignments for achievement at the highest levels. This book is also for appreciating you, finding self-acceptance and inspiration!

AUTHOR'S PHILOSOPHY

- As each of us is an individual we each have special needs that require differentiation of instruction.
- What we think and feel becomes what we say and do.
- Memory is formed from one's emotional involvement in experiences.
- We learn and teach simultaneously, and we're all teachers of something.
- Project- and performance-based learning situations allow for personal involvement and retention of material.
- In order for effective learning to occur, the educational setting must be a comfort zone for this shared environment.
- Conversation with others, self-appreciation, and instructional opportunities that involve the learner in self-efficacy provide viable opportunities for success—personal and academic.
- One classroom rule: No put downs . . . only lift ups!
- Through assignments that promote personal involvement, self-acceptance follows with the ingrained concept of "I am enough."

Part I

EXPLAINING THE INTERACTIVE METHOD (IM) REGARDING THINKING SKILLS, MEMORY, AND CLASSROOM IMPLEMENTATION

Chapter One

Explaining the Interactive Method (IM)

Experience-Based Teaching and Learning

The Child That Dreams
I am still the child
And, I shall spend these years
In wandering and dreaming
Of what I have not, but wish
For and could be.
And, you shall teach me
So that I may grow
With truth and knowledge
To become the person
Within my being
Who will turn one day
To teach another
Who is still the child that dreams.

—M. S. Schiering (1967)

This chapter begins with a poem that's followed by 16 questions regarding a personal reflection on that piece. Then, there are paragraphs that explain "different abilities" and "special needs." There's information about "labeling" students and a suggestion for eradicating this with an alteration of one's thinking. An explanation of the Interactive Method (IM) is provided with the components of the IM being the Interactive Book Report (IBR), Activity-Based Learning Center (ABLC), and Project- and/or Performance-Based Learning (P/PBL). After each of the aforementioned components are given attention, there is a closing with "Journal and/or Discussion Questions."

POEM: THE CHILD THAT DREAMS: REFLECTION QUESTIONS

After reading the above poem, what are you thinking? Does it make you wonder if you're still the child who dreams? If so, about what did you dream? If you had a career aspiration, what was it? Did you see teaching in your future? Why or why not? If you were not a dreamer, what were you like when you were a child? What was of significance to you? Did grades/test scores matter? And if so, in what way? Did you do well or not so well academically? Why do you suppose that was the case? What type of teaching style did your teachers practice? What did you like about school or any classroom? How do you suppose the teacher's way of teaching impacted your learning? Why?

ANALYSIS

Your answers to these 16 questions about a poem addressing your past aspirations probably had an impact on you becoming a teacher. This author knows the answers she had . . . her dreams influenced her decision about this profession. But more importantly, the answers affected "how" she chose to teach and learn. That beginning teaching was in Ohio a long while ago. The memories of those years inspired this author's present-day teaching and learning.

Who cares? What does that matter? What's important about that for me? The answers to those questions may determine whether you're open to the idea of there being different ways for different abilities and special needs student learners. But let's not jump forward too fast. First, let's take a look at what the differences are between these two labeled types of students.

Is there a difference between different abilities and special needs? While the former indicates one's capabilities, the latter refers to one's necessities. In any heterogeneous classroom, there is a mixture of these types of student learners. You have, commonly, those who work above, at, and below grade level, as well as those who require more instruction, due to learning insufficiencies. This last type of learner is often considered "at risk."

Overall, instructional methods that work for one group or individual may not work for another. That may seem as obvious as the idea of needing to reach students before we can teach them. But if not, the following pages of this chapter and book finitely provide methods and techniques that engage student learners. This is by first comprehending their situation and/or trying different ways to guide and/or instruct them.

Special needs students are often regarded as those with learning disabilities or difficulties. But it should be noted that those who are considered "gifted" also fall into this category. How do you suppose those ability differences are determined? It could be by variance in test scores, a physical alteration among the assembled, or something else. Within each of these aforementioned groups there are varied levels of aptitudes. While some above grade level student learners are exceptional in several subject areas, they may be "at" grade level in others. Or there are students who are gifted and have special needs or disabilities in varied subject areas, simultaneously.

Subsequently, "different abilities" are part of each classroom, and each of us, this author thinks, has "special needs" of one sort or another, whether academic, social, physical, or emotional, at one time or another. In order to teach our students, we first need to be aware of their strengths and aptitudes as well as areas of difficulty. In order to reach students, we need to know each one academically and what constitutes his or her emotional perspectives/social cognition attitudes regarding learning and the classroom in general.

"DIFFERENT ABILITIES" AND "SPECIAL NEEDS" LABELING

It seems that, as a society, we readily accept our children in the academic arena as having exceptionalities. Both of the terms *different abilities* and especially *special needs* carry a negative connotation, as they refer to those who might fail in a particular subject area or at a certain grade level. These students are "different" than the rest of the class's students, where "being different" isn't good. "Fitting-in" is good!

What if we stopped pigeonholing these learners into categories that emphasize what's wrong and focused on the "strengths" of these learners? Or what if we, as educators, started saying what the learner can do, as opposed to what he or she can't do? And perhaps we could find alternative means of instruction and assessment or differentiated instruction to assist these students in their learning endeavors.

The student who excels or works above grade level is also one who comes under a title of "special needs." In a manner of speaking, this giftedness is a "disability," while at the same time it is not one. The reason these persons are in the special needs category is because they are "different" from classmates in that they excel in learning. There's also the "twice exceptional" student who excels in some areas and does poorly in others. Comparisons are made in the classroom by teachers and students alike. Subsequently, this author reiterates the idea of addressing students' strengths, as opposed to learning difficulties.

IN THE PAST: TEACHING STRATEGIES

At one time, and even in some schools today, there was, for the most part, a philosophy that students were to be passive recipients of information. This was called then, and now, the Socratic method. Prior to adulthood and even on into it, at the advanced levels of education a "seen and not heard" attitude was exhibited. Well, not everywhere, but it could be considered a mainstay in the school setting and sometimes in the home.

So what? You may ask, as this method isn't followed now . . . or is it? How much "say" do students have in "how" an assignment is done? Do they use their imagination? Do they decide "when" something is to be taught or for "how long"? Do they choose a partner or work alone? Who determines these factors? In most cases, it's the teacher who is the decision-maker. This type of teaching is referred to as teacher centered, as opposed to student centered. The latter of these takes into consideration the abilities and needs of all students in a classroom and focuses on that.

Yet another factor regarding the use of most teaching methods, other than the IM, is the idea that psychologists call "functional fixedness" (Mlodinow, December 2018), which involves patterned thinking. This is thinking in a particular sequence or way that has an order to it or a pattern that does not vary. It well might not apply to using one's imagination or involving a learner in thinking "outside the box," because a teacher imposes a set of "rules," as opposed to "guidelines." The inability to think in new ways affects people in every corner of society.

So functional fixedness is not limited to the classroom, but it may commence there with "how things are to be done" being imposed on learners. It's like being unmoving or "trapped" in a way of thinking that disallows the aforementioned flexibility of the IM. What is important about the involvement of students in their own learning is that they take ownership of it and may view it from a "beginner's mind" (Mlodinow on Zen Buddhist philosophy). Such a mind-set involves having a new perspective about a former one.

In some ways, the IM is like the difference between convergent and divergent questions. Convergent questions are closed and fact based. There is only one answer that is correct. Such a question may be exemplified by asking who was the U.S. president after George Washington? However, divergent questions are open ended and allow for one's thinking to impact an answer. There's no one way to do something but many, depending on the person doing the task, project, performance, or producing a product. A divergent question on the same topic might be, "What are good qualities of a leader?"

One other important factor is that with the IM, because student learners are actively involved in "doing" an assignment, because they are engaged, the material being addressed is readily recalled. Furthermore, information is retained for a long period of time. Just as the questions addressing the poem at the beginning of this chapter called for recall of one's childhood, so too does the IM, with its three major components (discussed in the next section) allow for remembering.

This recall of information, which later may be on a test or part of a discussion, is made possible due to motor and mind memory being in play. As opposed to listening to a book or lecture or memorizing material that's presented in various media formats, or through only the auditory and visual modalities, it is the involvement in "experiencing" that creates and sustains memories.

Dewey's Experientialism in 1937, which later became Constructivism, or Dales's *Cone of Experience* from the 1940s refer to a 90% retention rate for material that is learned by "doing." Apprenticeship programs were ones where tradesmen taught novices how to do carpentry, coopering, sewing, printing, and 29 other skills by having the apprentice practice what was to be accomplished. Again, it is the physical and mental memory that is so intertwined that one recalls readily what has been taught and, subsequently, learned.

THE INTERACTIVE METHOD: DIFFERENTIATION OF INSTRUCTION: EXPERIENCE-BASED LEARNING

The concepts of differentiating instruction are primarily referenced in this book as being interactive learning that involves "educational gaming" and also involves instructional techniques that involve projects with resulting products or performances. The major component of the IM is that it involves learning that's adaptable to the students with respect to their being the deciders of "how" something will be done. This, of course is within the parameters of a specified topic in a specified discipline, which is known as the "curriculum."

The IM addresses the "how" in the preceding paragraph with the understanding that a "method" is a way of doing something. There's a set pattern, but in the case of the IM, there's a great deal of flexibility in that pattern. This is seen in Chapters 4 through 9 of this book. Overall, the IM requires communication, a taking in and giving out of information and activities being designed and implemented to call for personal involvement in the process of learning.

Differentiation of Instruction

Differentiation of instruction and providing student engagement in learning experiences are two of the major components of the IM. It's for all students! Most importantly, the IM covers a broad spectrum of instructional techniques. Its approach "engages" students who're learning through inventing for the purposes of being creative, sharing ideas, and exchanging visions while being interactive, oftentimes through the development of this type of instructional resource.

Hands-On Instruction

Aside from what has already been presented, you're invited to think about the idea that the IM stands for a means of learning and teaching that addresses one's doing "hands-on" types of work. Additionally, it addresses in detail being creatively and imaginatively involved in the cognitive/thinking process, so much so that critical and creative thinking are at their zenith.

The overall idea of these varied types of instruction or differentiation is that students partake in their own learning.

Flexibility

The IM is "flexible" in that the learner decides how the components may be done or a project or performance may be accomplished. Subsequently, that flexibility of having no specific parameters, other than the end product, allows for (1) research being able to be conducted, (2) watching others work on an assignment, (3) making changes to one's own perspective and/or design, as well as (4) being present for the demonstration of work done with positive feedback provided.

Teacher Question: Camaraderie

In the IM classroom, when an assignment is completed, the teacher asks the class, "What did you like about this classmate's or these classmates' work?" This question invites uplifting statements. Subsequently, class members come to accept and appreciate one another's efforts. There is a camaraderie that ensues because of acknowledgment of one's own work being recognized by peers in a complimentary way.

The IM serves as a guide for performance tasks that include the inspiration for divergent (open-ended) thinking, use of imagination, and promoting independent learning but also involves design planning, with a finished product, and builds on prior experience or obtaining it through multimedia research. Since many activities are done not by one's self but in a partnership or a small group, there's classroom "interaction" and "collaboration-with-peers" learning, "self-assessment," and "self-reliance," as well as the building of a positive classroom community. Student learners come to appreciate the differences in how one obtains and retains information by being involved in the learning process and observing classmates achieving goals using different ways.

THE IM'S "THINKING" FACTOR

Reciprocity

With the IM, attention to identification and use of specific thinking skills is seen on the Reciprocal Thinking: Cognition to Metacognition Chart (Schiering, 1999). This hierarchical and simultaneously imposed set of thinking skills goes from beginning cognitive functions such as comparing and contrasting to the metacognitive processes of recall, reflection, and self-actualization. The introduction of the Reciprocal Thinking Phases is in the first book of this series and is readdressed in this book's second chapter.

THE IM'S THREE MAJOR ACTIVITY-BASED COMPONENTS

1. An *Interactive Book Report (IBR)* has its educational games or interactive instructional resources in the five major disciplines of reading, ELA, math, science, and social studies, as well as a creative game-type page. These are preceded by a title page, author review, summary of a story or topic, Reciprocal Thinking Chart, and a welcome page or an invitation to play the pages of the IBR.
2. *Activity-Based Learning Center (ABLC)* oftentimes is the taking of pages from an IBR and making them poster size, or at least larger than notebook paper size. These are placed in an area of the classroom, fastened to a trifold board or placed on tables, where one or a group of students may go when others are receiving more formal instruction. The area where the trifold boards are located or tables with pages or activities one would find in an IBR are referred to as an ABLC. ABLC examples are in Chapter 8.
3. *Project- and/or Performance-Based Learning (P/PBL)* activities call for a product through the "project" portion of it, then address a displaying or presenting of the product. This is like the IBR's interactive pages in that there is the construction of something. But P/PBL might also entail research that is then conducted in a performance-style display, as opposed to making a game-type activity and presenting it. The interaction comes in the gathering of information and putting something together for a performance or sharing. The close of Chapter 10 in the series' first book and in Chapter 9 of this book are examples of P/PBL.

At its core, a performance enables learners to demonstrate their knowledge aptitude by creating and producing a project or product, as well as providing a demonstration of these or partaking in a performance on a discipline-specified topic. These tasks allow for the use of real-life situations, rather than just providing information on a philosophy. With that in mind, the following are some projects that may be done with a resultant performance:

Projects

These may include educational games, interactive instructional resources, graphic organizers involving decision-making; varied types of books; drawings; advertisement posters; bulletin boards; exhibitions; science experiments; computer, board, or wall games; acrostic or other types of poems; letters; word-family foam-core board displays; brochures with instructions or information and illustrations; dioramas; three-dimensional displays; and diagrams (Schiering, 1996, 2015).

Performances

These are a few that would be considered a performance: poetry competition, game show, mock radio, television or video broadcast, demonstration of a specific discipline teaching lesson, mock television or radio broadcast, play or role play, speech, video-clip interview or informational piece related to a topic such as weather, demonstration of a game made or something involving cooking or a craft project, debate, and storytelling (Schiering, 1996, 2015; McTighe & Wiggins, 1999).

JOURNAL AND/OR DISCUSSION QUESTIONS

1. How would you explain the differences between abilities and needs?
2. What is meant by "labeling" student learners?
3. What might one do to eliminate the labeling of learners?
4. How would you describe the IM?
5. What is the connection between the IM, differentiation of instruction, and experiential learning?
6. What are the three components of the IM, and how do these apply to all types of learners?

Chapter Two

Reciprocal Thinking, Cognitive Collective, and Memories

The Teaching of Thinking

This chapter focuses on one's thinking/cognitive skills. With definitions and explanations, you are led along a Nine-Step Pathway to the use of the components of the Interactive Method (IM) for memory acquisition and the teaching of thinking. Of course, this is for students with different abilities and/or special needs, with the realization that we are each a member of one, and possibly both, of those categories.

It is very important to note that in this chapter, there is explicit explanation regarding the identification of what one is thinking. There is also information on feelings and these being different from thinking. Rumination is given attention as "functional fixedness." The hierarchy and reciprocity of thinking are addressed in Figure 2.1, "Reciprocal Thinking Phases: Cognition and Metacognition," with several explanatory paragraphs following the figure.

At the close of the "pathway" topics/headings, there is the teaching of thinking using the IM's components involving experiential learning with identification of what thinking skills were applied when playing the pages of an Interactive Book Report (IBR). These illustrations address thinking skills relating to (1) interactive instructional resources/different ways for the IM's three components and (2) the Reciprocal Thinking Identification Illustration Chart for Storytelling. The chapter closes with "Journal and/or Discussion Questions."

THE TEACHING OF THINKING

Before getting into the Nine-Step Pathway regarding memory acquisition and the teaching of thinking, this author explains that by being able to identify what one is thinking, thinking is happening. That seems like a relatively obvious concept. However, when one makes an interactive instructional resource or there is a project and/or performance-based assignment, there is thinking that is required to do that assignment. The Reciprocal Thinking Phases Chart gives the student learner the finite opportunity to use thinking. This may be for designing and creating an activity or performing. Each involves decision-making and problem-solving as well as so many other cognitive and metacognitive skills by "doing" an assignment. The person doing and observing the finished product is being taught thinking just by his or her involvement in it. When one realizes that involvement, there is awareness of the teaching of thinking being viable.

PATHWAY STEP #1: THINKING/COGNITION

Just for clarification, this sentence relates that *thinking* and *cognition* mean the same thing. These words are synonyms. Truth be known, we're always involved in thinking processes, whether accompanied with language usage or not. On the flip side of always thinking is that act of identification of what we're thinking customarily being bypassed as a nonnecessity or something we simply don't consciously address regularly, if at all.

As children in our households, the idea of not thinking but rather following directions might well be practiced. Yet in some households, children are taught to think positively and even question everything. In school, depending on the teacher, students may be instructed to be quiet and not interrupt and be part of Chapter 1's Socratic method. Or the student is only asked about what he or she might be thinking when it seems appropriate for the teacher to get a few responses. Actually, as student learners and well after that, we become accustomed to, or "reflectively speaking" notice, the "habit" to not think about what we are thinking.

We may have a sense of being "stuck" when thinking about a particular thing. This is when rumination is evident in that we can't get a particular phrase out of our mind or something someone did or said remains with us to the point of annoyance. But that is not thinking about thinking. That is functional fixedness, as referenced in this book's Chapter 1. Such dwelling on one thought is rumination, which is akin to chewing a piece of gum far after it has lost its flavor. Ugh!

This "being trapped" cognitively, with one or a series of thoughts, does not help with reflection but hinders it. Recall and reflection are metacognitive processes that the IM encourages and result in self-actuation, which is the making of the pages of an Interactive Book Report (IBR) or sections of an Activity-Based Learning Center (ABLC) or activities of a Project- and/or Performance-Based Learning (P/PBL). But more on that later.

In the overall scope of things, this idea of *thinking and knowing what is being thought* may be seen as time-consuming and as a process that requires training. Still, we are always thinking, even while resting. At that time, it's called dreaming. Dreams are a reflection of thoughts, ideas, opinions, judgments, and even feelings. Definitions of these appear later in this chapter.

There and Here: Thinking Topics

In the first book of this two-book series, prelanguage thinking is examined in Chapter 7. Definitions of specific thinking skills with examples of each one are in Chapter 9. However, in this second book, the present chapter has an overview of thinking and presentation of the chart and aforementioned other figures, with a small commentary following each of these.

Consideration

Consider this: In fact, we're not accustomed to thinking about what we are thinking. For example, your friend might show you a picture of him or her skateboarding, in a swimming competition, having lunch with cousins, a forest, a flower, and so forth. The thought you have might be as simple as "good skateboarding . . . nice flower." No further thought is necessarily given unless conversation about the picture is expected. At that juncture, the thinking is done for the purpose of what to say more than analysis of the image shown to you or you naturally thinking more deeply.

Think and Feel: Say and Do

This author has long stated that "what we think and feel becomes what we say and do" (2015, 40), and the following Figure 2.1 introduces you not only to the hierarchical structure but most profoundly to the "reciprocity" of thinking. After the figure, each phase is explained in a paragraph. The chart is used as a guide to stimulate thinking by recognizing what thinking is occurring and that thinking within and between phases becomes evident.

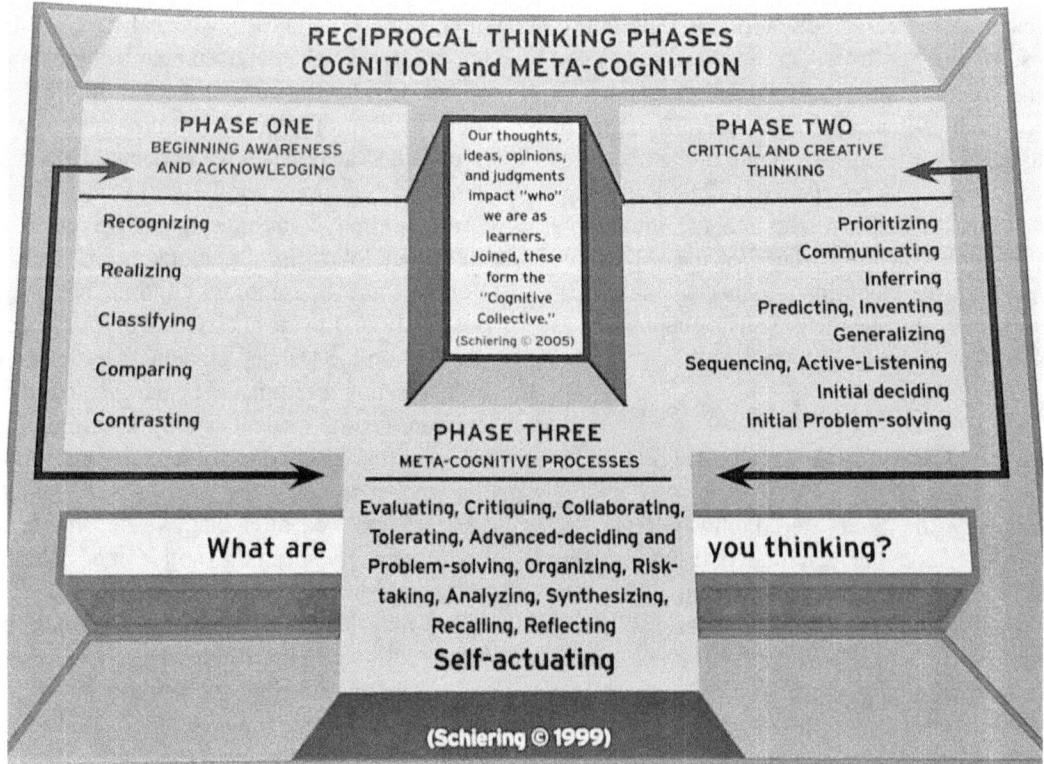

Figure 2.1. Reciprocal Thinking Phases: Cognition and Metacognition

PATHWAY STEP #2:
RECIPROCITY OF THINKING HISTORY

Reciprocity of thinking refers to the ongoing exchange of cognitive skill usage that forms memory. Each of the following thinking phases in Figure 2.1 originally came from this author's doctoral dissertation in 1999. It was modified in 2003, where it became a paradigm within a model for academic and social cognition (see Appendix A, Raynor & Armstrong et al., 2003). In this "model," thinking and feeling were joined to form the *Cognitive Collective*. This exemplar addressed thinking and feeling impacting individuals' learning with respect to the formation of thoughts, ideas, opinions, and judgments in coexistence with sensory or emotional responses to stimuli.

Thinking and feelings were and are visualized as the basis for "belief and values" as well as "common social and societal realities" (Raynor & Armstrong et al., 2003). This author has come to teach, through research done on the reciprocity of thinking, about how knowing what one is thinking helps to clarify learning. This is accomplished with the individual's acknowledgment of the finite identification of the cognitive and metacognitive skills being experienced at any time. What you are thinking may not be what I am thinking, but awareness of what is transpiring, cognitively, empowers learners and teachers alike regarding understanding.

Overall View of Reciprocal Thinking Phases

The reciprocity of thinking refers to the ongoing exchange of cognitive skills that ultimately results in the formation of memory. This exchange occurs within and between the Phases of Beginning Awareness, Critical and Creative Thinking, and the Metacognitive Processes, as seen in Figure 2.1. As mentioned above, what you are thinking may not be what I am thinking, but awareness of what is transpiring, cognitively, empowers learners and teachers alike. How? This is accomplished by knowing what one is thinking. Realizing this assists the individual in clarifying his or her learning with acknowledging the finite identification of the cognitive and metacognitive skills being experienced at any given moment.

The use of the word *reciprocal* in the title "Reciprocal Thinking Phases" demonstrates that the processes of cognition and metacognition are occurring simultaneously, as opposed to being developmental, with one evolving from the other. The use of the word *reciprocal* emphasizes that thinking is ongoing and conducted within and between the phases. The movement between and within phases is occurring naturally, as one does not purposefully go from one thinking skill to another; it just happens. With respect to the three components of the IM, the beauty of these named and defined skills is in the individual's identification that what one is thinking assists in the learning and retention process while "doing" an activity. As Descartes wrote, "I think; therefore, I am."

PATHWAY STEP #3:
EXPLANATION OF PHASES

Phase I: Basic Awareness and Acknowledging

This first reciprocal phase involves skill development relating to fact-finding and ordering techniques. These include initial classification and cause the learner to start making connections to personal experiences and those presented orally or in written formats. Learners are able to respond to various stimuli in conversations as well as configure answers to literal comprehension questions with accuracy. This phase takes into consideration an individual's earliest forms of awareness with recognizing, realizing, classifying, comparing, and contrasting.

Phase II: Critical and Creative Thinking

This phase involves the transcendence and inclusion through movement from and within one's beginning awareness, as much as within and between the third phase. In this second phase, learners process skills through visualizing and verbalizing the connections they have made from personal prior experiences and/or read material or verbalizations of others. It can be determined that the combination of critical and creative thinking relies on past awareness to construct new meaning.

Skills in this phase include such factors as the ability to prioritize by placing a level of importance on ideas or materialistic things. Then there is communicating, which this author emphasizes as being the act of talking "with" someone, as opposed to "at" or "to" others. There are also thinking skills regarding inferring, predicting, generalizing, sequencing, and initial deciding coupled with problem-solving.

The learner may hypothesize, imagine, or visualize making connections from his or her own experiences or reading material for applied comprehension. Subsequently, determining outcomes from actions taken provides a comprehensive set of thoughts for problem-solving, a matter that is addressed as a metacognitive process.

In this second phase, there is also discernment with critical thinking, as well as predicting, and initial decision-making by not accepting an answer or idea at face value. One final thing about this second phase is that its title, "Critical and Creative Thinking," when analyzed, connotes that in order to be creative, one employs critical thinking on an ongoing basis. (In the first book in this series, there are two figures addressing *linear* and *creative thinking* for a finite examination of creative processes for different individuals.)

Phase III: Metacognitive Processes

This phase occurs when the thinking goes beyond the cognitive and the learner actually knows what he or she wants to realize—exhibiting a control over his or her intake and output of information. There is critiquing accompanied by self-actuation through evaluation, and synoptic exercises (general and summative overviews) occur. There is a realization of action or actions that need to be taken to facilitate the acquisition of knowledge. Metacognition is domain dependent as it is instantiated (firmly grounded) in a context or learning task (Tobias & Everson, 1995).

This "being grounded" refers to learning that addresses a specific subject area and references students' working in a format that is structured and sequential. Abedi and O'Neil (1996) defined *metacognition* as consisting of strategies for planning, monitoring or self-checking cognitive/affective strategies, and self-awareness.

The metacognitive processes in Phase III are realized through evaluating, organizing, critiquing, collaborating, tolerating, deciding, risk taking, inventing, analyzing, synthesizing, advanced problem-solving, recalling, reflecting, and self-actualizing. This last skill is when someone goes forth and does something, such as is experienced using the IM.

The result of learners and teachers' identifying and implementing the higher order thinking skills in this Phase III is clearly evident in the area of implied comprehension with regard to their ability to address this type of thinking. Or ask and answer this implied or conceptualized type of question, which relies on one's interpretation of context clues that are written, observed, or verbalized. Additionally, the implication may come from tactile and/or kinesthetic involvement. These clues lead one to think that a specific answer is viable, more so that another one. An example would be a sentence about seeing a dog's footprints on the sand. It's implied that previously this animal had walked on the sand, because of these footprints.

PATHWAY STEP #4: TWO PARTS OF THE RECIPROCAL THINKING PHASES (RTP)

Now that you've seen Figure 2.1 and read about each phase, this author relates that it is important to note that the RTP actually has two displayed processes. The first or most easily seen is the "hierarchical" one. Movement goes in stages; specifically, you see that there are low, intermediate, and high levels of thinking. With this visualization, it would appear that one thinks in stages and can't go to a higher level of thinking until he or she has experienced a lower level. But that is not the case for the reciprocity of thinking!

The second part, not so easily seen or imagined, in the RTP is the simultaneous processing of information. What that means is that thinking takes place concurrently and instantaneously *within* and *between* phases. There is *no* set age, stage, or developmental experience that occurs prior to one phase or another.

PATHWAY STEP #5: EXPLAINING THINKING AND FEELINGS

Many times as we speak or write, we use the words *I think* and *I feel* interchangeably. Pause in your reading for a moment now and ask yourself what you're thinking and feeling. Is there a difference? If so, what's that difference? This author answering those questions thought, "I'm thinking that I'd bet most people don't see these words as having a different meaning. I feel uncomfortable with that awareness."

Well, from research this author has conducted, she notes that there's a difference between thinking and feeling. These words are not the same, and neither are the actions of each one. While one's thinking may impact his or her feeling and vice versa to the point of not knowing which is which, they are different entities. The following definitions of thinking skills and feelings may assist in clarification of this anomaly, as presented in the first of these companion books and before that by Schiering and Bogner (2008, 2011).

1. *Thoughts:* Immediate conscious responses to reflection that involve memory. *Reflection* is further defined by Schon (1997) as having two forms, which are reflection "in" action, or thoughts occurring now in the present, and reflection "on" action, as referencing something that happened in the past. *Example:* From my experience, I have thoughts that focus on learning's being multidimensional.
2. *Ideas:* A prediction of future responses or speculation based on one's perspective as a result of reflection. *Example:* She thought about what she'd read and got the idea about good teaching practices being something on which she'd focus.
3. *Opinions:* A combination of thoughts and ideas such that a formulated concept results. *Example:* The teachers were asked for their reaction to the curriculum

and gave a two-page written response regarding the importance of student engagement in learning.
4. *Judgments:* Concretized thoughts, ideas, and opinions that are impacted by memory while being based on reflection concerning past experiences. Oftentimes based on one's level of attachment to a situation, judgments are not easily changed, but they *can* change. If they are easily modified, then you've expressed a thought, idea, or opinion, as opposed to a judgment. *Example:* My judgment concerning eye color is that green is the most attractive.
5. *Feelings:* A sensory and/or emotional response to stimuli that may be descriptive or classificatory. *Example:* The water felt soft as it slid through my open fingers.

Feelings are also defined as being the quality that something has in that one responds in a way that connotes feelings of an emotional or intuitive nature and/or reflects on something to establish a formed response that is grounded in thought, ideas, opinions, and judgments. *Example:* The music collectively evoked the audience's strong sense of joy as the symphony began.

Subsequently, feelings and emotions are one and the same and yet can be observed or defined as being joined. These then are transrational responses to stimuli in that a sensory response to situations occurs at the same juncture as deeply held thoughts, ideas, opinions, and judgments. Bogner and Schiering (2007) refer to feelings and emotions as being "root responses" to stimuli.

PATHWAY STEP #6: THE COGNITIVE COLLECTIVE

Human beings think as well as feel. The result is that this unity of thinking and feeling happens within the classroom as well as outside it. Throughout the day, individuals move between varying cognitive processes and emotions. As teachers, we must address this natural progression and interplay by recognizing, first, that they occur, and second, that in order to be effective teachers or human beings, we must know how this process happens and attend to it. The Cognitive Collective is the interplay between and within an individual's or a whole group's thinking and feelings.

Reciprocity of Thinking and Feelings

Basically, this author posits that all learning has reciprocity of thinking and feelings. Our life experiences, not the number of them but the actual experience and at any age, impact our thinking and feelings. She states in the first book in this series, "If the emotional/feeling experience was significant, then it will be recalled for a long time to come" (Schiering 2014b). And one other thought is that our cognitive and metacognitive abilities and feeling reactions increase in number and depth along with the amount and/or accumulation of experiences we have. The toddler's thinking is simplistic in nature but becomes more complex as he or she matures. That is an example of human nature.

Thinking Complexity

Thinking occurs in varying phases of complexity that are reciprocal in nature with the individual's moving seamlessly between and among them. Each individual's thinking can be characterized by a number of specific cognitive skills that can be identified by individuals. This being the case, one can hone and develop these skills, identifying when he or she is using each and becoming more proficient in its usage.

Tasks for the learner and the teacher, therefore, would seem to be attending directly to helping one "know what he/she is thinking," helping each learner to identify when he or she is using a particular skill and assisting them in developing mastery over it. (Schiering et al., 2011)

Additionally, thinking certainly involves the act of withholding judgment in order to use past knowledge and experience to find new information, concepts, or conclusions. To think critically, one moves from guessing to estimating, grouping to classifying, supposing to hypothesizing, and having opinions based on reason. Thinking is truly a complex process.

Feeling Complexity

Ask yourself the following question and then configure an answer: "Does one have to experience feeling bad to know feeling good?" Hmm, that's a complex question, as it evidences not just how one might feel but upon reflection, thinking as well. As stated earlier, sometimes thinking and feeling are intertwined. The Cognitive Collective, as you may recall, is the combination of thinking and feeling. Still, when it comes to just feeling, does one have to experience the opposite of a particular feeling to know what is felt?

This author has asked college classes semester after semester what they think is the answer to the previous paragraph's question. The answers have been, interestingly, twofold. The overall response to the question is, "No. One does not have to experience feeling bad in order to realize feeling good." And that is because feelings are identified by emotional or sensory reactions to a circumstance. One just "feels" good or bad or comfortable or uncomfortable.

Students have continued with how feelings are just as complex as thinking. And yet there is a difference in that feeling something is a physical and/or expressive response to stimuli. Subsequently, if you walk into a room where you don't know anyone, you may feel uncomfortable, as indicated by you shaking or having a nervous sensory response. On the other hand, you might feel elated that you don't know anyone in the room. Your body and emotions match. Feeling oftentimes relies on a sensation that is experienced without thinking.

The converse answer to the question about needing to know bad to feel good has sometimes been answered with a yes. However, this author suggests that at such a time, thinking is tremendously involved. You may have had a previous experience in entering a room where you know no one. The thinking you did on that occasion will impact how you feel now, whether good or bad. So in one instance, it is your body that influences how you feel and in another, your mind and body together. Feeling is as complex as thinking and as interwoven.

PATHWAY STEP #7:
INFORMATION REGARDING MEMORY

How do you suppose memories are best formed? Or why do you remember some things and forget other things? Searching one's thoughts, ideas, or opinions, it would seem evident that there was some emotional attachment to cause one to recall a situation. Reflection on a topic brings back memories, due to many factors, but the most significant is that there was enough of an experience to retain the information surrounding the topic or incident.

For example, this author can vividly recall her dad reading poetry in the living room's brown velvet chair. While she didn't necessarily understand the poem, the significance of the situation of being read to by her dad was very large. One poem she recalls had the stanza "Laugh and the world laughs with you, weep and you weep alone. People want full measure of your pleasure, but they do not want your woe" (Wilcox, 1952, 1).

Interestingly, she also remembers riding her first horse and the name of the person who taught her, Borby. That's because she went on to love riding and entered competitions in her teenage years. In early adulthood, she bought her first horse and rode every day after teaching school. Another memory that began in childhood was learning to ice skate and do twirls. Each experience is recalled vividly because of the magnitude of her involvement in it. What are some things you remember?

Much like modeling clay, one's brain changes, and the result is that the behaviors one has are altered. The previous behaviors experienced may be returned to, although not in exactly the same way. This ongoing and continual reconfiguring of the brain and mind results in what are called *memories*.

PATHWAY STEP #8:
WHAT MEMORY INVOLVES

All memory involves thinking—the ability of the brain to process, store, retrieve, and retain information, which is comprehension. For example, you are involved in making an interactive learning resource in science for a classroom project. So you decide to work with a classmate and design and construct a three-dimensional poster displaying the metamorphosis of a caterpillar.

What you do might be part of an IBR, ABLC, or P/PBL. You need the materials to construct the poster, and before that you need information from the internet or a science book about the stages of the caterpillar's development. You process the information and begin creating the display until the assigned date for presenting the finished project has arrived. Basically, you have *retained*, *processed*, *stored*, and *retrieved* information until it could be put into practice. And while you have experienced each of those processes, you have comprehended what was needed to do each one. That comprehension becomes part of your memory as you are constructing the poster.

The poster displays *literal* or *fact-based* understanding about each stage of the caterpillar's life cycle as depicted on the poster. Then, there is *applied* comprehension when one's response to that poster is given with knowing about this life cycle and perhaps how this differs from the human life process. Such differences may include childhood, tweenhood, teen hood, young adulthood, and so on . . . depending where one is in that process. The idea is that the poster on the animal's life cycle has been applied to that of humans in stages experienced.

Lastly, there is *implied* comprehension. This is the response to indirect evidence that leads a person to think something is going to happen without directly stating that. For the life cycle poster, this would be what's observed with the stages' context regarding the question, "What happens next?" As a result of looking at the poster and the stages, and while it's not directly stated or shown, one would think that "death" is the final stage.

One's comprehension influences beliefs and values, actions and reactions an individual takes or has for learning through experience. Comprehension may be shared for comparing and contrasting to past thinking or another's ideas on a topic. What is understood becomes part of who one is, as *comprehension forms personality, ability, accountability, and adaptability* to learning endeavors, or a lack of this last skill. And ultimately, comprehension involves use of one's memory, which comes in the three following forms:

1. *Attention:* The ability to focus on a specific stimulus without being distracted.
    Example: We used the IM for the making of task cards for one activity on an ABLC on life cycles of a caterpillar, frog, bird, and horse. There was one set of cards for each animal's life cycle.
2. *Orientation:* The ability to be aware of self and certain realities and facts that manipulate the information. These are commensurate with the ability of a person to respond to stimuli and align with everyday life experiences.
    Example: When making the task cards in a small-group format, one class had five persons making four cards each for life cycle. It was noted that other groups were working on different self-corrective materials. These all were about the same life cycles topic but in a different format. Flash cards were one of these. And another group did "matching" on the computer. Overall, the comments were that most liked the task card way of doing the life cycles. This was because they thought they recognized learning from these by manipulating the cards to match the shapes and using them in their own time frame. A contribution was related that one reason for liking these was that each person was in charge of his or her learning and liked that groupmates contributed to this activity. Basically, what was related was that the group members learned from each other by using each other's task cards. And the collaboration was excellent.
3. *Decision-making and problem-solving:* The ability to understand a problem, generate a solution or two, and evaluate these.
    Example: The Decision-Making/Critical-Thinking Graphic Organizer is explained in Chapter 9 and shown in Figure 9.5. In the first book in this series, Jerry Redondo (2018) addresses career paths he was considering. These included being a firefighter, teacher/professor, or police officer. He selected the middle one after listing his thoughts regarding possible positives and negatives of each profession. His final decision related that his selection was based on his love of children and making a positive impact on their lives, as represented by his own love of learning.

Factoid on Memory

The most fundamental things scientists have learned about memory is that we do not store memories whole and therefore do not retrieve them that way either. When we remember something, we actually reconstruct it by combining elements of the original experience. (Brandt, 1999, 235–238)

PATHWAY STEP #9: THE TEACHING OF THINKING AND THE IM: EXAMPLES

Of utmost importance is acknowledging that one of the most important by-products of the IM is that those using it, through its components, are continually involved in metacognition. As stated in Step #1 and repeated here, *metacognition is the act of consciously thinking about one's thinking*. Making and/or using the IBR, ABLC, P/PBL or being involved in experiential learning results in an analysis of (1) what is being thought, (2) what ideas are present, (3) what opinions are held, and (4) what judgments are made, along with (5) how one feels about the interaction, designing and creating with thinking critically, and (6) being prepared for tests that address the subjects of the interactive learning resources.

As explained in the first book of this two-book series "In order for one to teach thinking, the process of 'observation' is important, but more important is knowledge of the Reciprocal Thinking Phases: Cognition and Metacognition and how the skills within this figure apply to thinking" (Schiering, 2017–present). They apply through the use of them. And then, metacognitively, there is the identification of them with awareness and further implementation and explanation as to how each is being addressed. Such exposure and application allows one to comprehend his or her thinking and purposes of it, regardless of location or ability level.

The author paraphrases and synthesizes material from her 2015 *Learning and Teaching Creative Cognition* publication: The IM and accompanying components serve as a constant for the act of recalling, using one's memory, and having experiential learning that results in retention of material. In turn, this retention of material connects with making and using that retention via the IBR, ABLC or P/PBL, or any interactive instructional resource. Of course, the retention assists with recall for tests as well.

It is primarily the act of experiencing the components of the IM that lead one to remember the content material in the interaction and bring it forth for future use and development. Components are used to help study and explore information that has been researched or simply presented. The two forthcoming examples are designed to show how recall is evidenced with use of two different charts that address thinking-skill identification for later application on one's own time.

"The Reciprocal Thinking skills are used for the *teaching of thinking*, through realization that specific cognitive and metacognitive skills are being utilized when activities are being made or played" (Schiering, 2016b, 13). *The mind-brain connection is functioning alongside tactile and kinesthetic involvement, which involves muscle memory.*

"Playing or doing the activities involves the highest level of metacognition, which is *self-actualizing*. And then again, that 'doing' involves the implementation of other thinking skills on the chart. In the following illustration there is an example of a portion of a Reciprocal Thinking Identification Chart for the playable pages of an IBR or activities for an ABLC. The chart is set up to have the name of the activities in the far left column and then corresponding thinking skills listed for each phase in the three columns to the right of the first one. This small excerpt shows only the thinking skills applied to the flip-chute. After perusing this chart made by Jill Guizzo (2018), there is a narrative, in several paragraphs, about how each thinking skill may be attributed to this specific activity.

Remember: IBR and ABLC activities are purposefully designed to involve the learner in metacognition!

EXPLANATION OF TEACHING THINKING: FLIP-CHUTE

The following explains how this Flip-Chute math activity was designed. The flip-chute cards had an illustrated addition problem on the top side. An example would be a picture of seven snails, all the same shape and color, and then two whales in black. The student would say, after putting the illustration side in the top slot, "Seven plus two equals nine," before the answer appeared coming out the bottom slot which would have that exact equation (7 + 2 = 9).

Twenty different addition illustrations and answer cards were provided for this activity. (What happens with a flip-chute card is that when placed in the upper slot, it turns upside down when going through the chute, so the answer comes out the bottom slot. When making a flip-chute card, the maker puts the question on the top side and then turns the card upside down and writes the answer. Subsequently, there is the question-in and answer-out of the flip-chute.)

An explanation of most of the thinking skills on the chart are now provided. *Recognizing* this type of question-in and answer-out process occurs when putting the flip-chute card into the upper slot. This beginning cognitive skill is also evident with *realizing* that the cards involve illustrated addition-type math equations. The equations were *classified* by illustration of the problem, with number answers emerging from the bottom slot. There was *comparing* the different equations when making a pile of the cards answered correctly and *contrasting* these to the ones that were not correctly addressed.

The three thinking skills from Phase II involved *inferring* that each card's top side would have an illustration, with the flip side being the actual equation. Also, *inferring* was evident when the answer was stated correctly that other answers would also be done correctly. This happened when the answer was said prior to the card's flip side, with the answer coming out through the bottom slot. *Inferring* the opposite might also have happened if answers were incorrect on a number of cards. *Sequencing* occurred when equations in illustrated and numbered responses became more complex. And *initial deciding* happened when the answer was given, mentally, before the answer on the card appeared.

The following thinking skills, Jill believed, were evidenced in Phase III. *Evaluating* the illustrations on the flip-chute card occurred when mentally *organizing* the number of snails and whales to be added. This was done by grouping shapes seen on the top side of the card. Follow-up of *evaluating* occurred with stating the answers in word format. *Analyzing* the illustrations being different occurred, with snails and whales as the pictured figures,

Activity Name	Phase I	Phase II	Phase III
Flip-Chute	Recognizing	Inferring	Evaluating
	Realizing	Sequencing	Organizing
	Classifying	Initial deciding	Analyzing
	Comparing		Recalling
	Contrasting		Advanced deciding
			Self-actualizing

such as the aforementioned example and others like three snails and four whales or five snails and two whales.

Recalling occurred when remembering what function was to be done—addition. And *recalling* and *advanced deciding* also happened when looking at the illustrations and converting these to numbers with respect to how the pictures stated the equation, what was to be added, and then stating the answer. *Self-actualizing* happened when placing the card in the top chute the correct way and "playing" this interactive instructional resource. And this highest metacognitive skill also happened when stating the equation and its answer.

EXPLANATION OF TEACHING THINKING: STORYTELLING

Teaching thinking with respect to storytelling is done on a Reciprocal Thinking Identification Chart. This is where the student learner identifies what thinking skills are used in the story being told. But first there is the writing of the story and then telling it to the class. This is a "slice-of-life story" . . . an experience that the student had at one time inside or outside school. The latter is preferred.

The aforementioned chart consists of fill-in sentences from the story or statements that relate to each of the thinking skills. Those fill-ins are to be read by the reader, stating the cognitive skill and then reading the statement. That is, realizing that this is a story about Sally and her fear of amusement parks, especially the roller coaster ride.

A Slice-of-Life Story

This is a story about Sally from the time she was a child and was afraid of the roller coaster ride at an amusement park. She'd been taken to this place by her parents with her older brother and sister when she was four or five. People screamed when they went on different types of rides. But no one feared the merry-go-round, and when she tried it, she loved it. This was primarily because she could see the ride wasn't fast and it went in a circle. The main reason she was scared of all rides except the merry-go-round was because they looked like they might upset her stomach. She'd seen people get sick after the roller coaster ride and people laughed when they saw this.

As years went by, she went to different amusement parks with family or friends. Some liked the roller coaster rides and other rides that Sally feared. And some didn't like the roller coaster ride. But Sally never actually went on any rides except the merry-go-round and one time the bumper cars. However, when first getting into the car, people bumped her into a corner and she thought, "Why do this again if I'm going to go nowhere?" As for other rides, her early childhood fears of either losing any food she'd eaten within the past few hours or simply dying from fright stayed with her. That she was afraid of heights added to this deep concern, and so she didn't try the Ferris wheel or anything that went up in the air.

As it turned out, when Sally was in her mid-20s, her husband, not knowing of her amusement park fear, suggested they have a "fun day" and go to Rye Beach. She was new to New York and didn't know this place, but thought, "Ah, sand and swimming, what fun!" She told her husband she'd be happy to have a day away from home, and she thought this was a great idea. Her husband had left off the last word of this destination. That word was *Play-land*. When she arrived there, Sally was immediately frozen in place with fear, as she saw this was an amusement park and not a beach. There were three big roller coaster rides directly in her line of vision, not to mention other scary rides.

Immediately, her husband suggested they go on one of the roller coaster rides. Not wanting him to know of her fear, she said, "I can't go on that ride because we're going to have a baby." He looked stunned and asked her when this blessed event was to take place. She shyly replied, "In a few years, I would hope." He paused before responding with, "I take it you're afraid of this ride . . . and other ones too?" She then admitted to being fearful of all amusement park rides except for the merry-go-round and explained that this had been the case since she was little. She further mentioned that she thought Rye Beach was a beach with sand and a swimming area. Since there was no beach and he'd not told her this place wasn't a beach, he suggested they go home and watch a movie. Sally wholeheartedly agreed.

Storytelling Chart

Phase I: Thinking Skills for Basic Awareness and Acknowledging	Identification of Skills Application: What's the Thinking?
Recognizing	This is a story about Sally and her lifelong fear of amusement park rides.
Realizing	Sally's fear paralyzed her.
Classifying	The types of rides at an amusement park
Comparing	Rides that would or might upset her stomach
Contrasting	The merry-go-round to other park rides
Phase II: Thinking Skills for Critical and Creative Thinking	**Identification of Skills Application: What's the Thinking?**
Prioritizing	Only the merry-go-round would be okay to ride.
Communicating	Sally would be happy to go away from home for a bit.
Inferring	She'd enjoy the sand and swimming at Rye Beach.
Active listening	Her husband's invitation to go to have a fun day
Predicting	Sally wouldn't go on a roller coaster ride.
Inventing	That she and her husband were going to have a baby
Generalizing	Other people may or may not like roller coasters.
Sequencing	Story events from Sally's young years to adulthood
Initial deciding	Not to try rides that might make her sick or die
Initial problem-solving	Avoid amusement parks, especially roller coasters.
Phase III: Thinking Skills for the Metacognitive Processes	**Identification of Skills Application: What's the Thinking?**
Evaluating	Why Sally avoided the Ferris wheel and other rides
Organizing	The sequence of events and reasons for each one
Critiquing	The characters' limited knowledge of one another
Collaborating	Having a "great idea" and "fun day" away from home
Tolerating	Sally's husband omitting the *Play-land* part of park title
Advanced deciding	To leave the amusement park and go home
Risk taking	Never before telling about fear of the roller coaster
Analyzing	How fear can paralyze someone's actions
Synthesizing	Packing 21 years into 10–20 minutes of storytelling
Advanced problem-solving	Sally not facing her fear by going on the roller coaster
Recalling	Sally's experiences concerning amusement park rides
Reflecting	Why there was a specific fear of roller coasters
Self-actualizing	Agree with husband and go home for movie

Source: Schiering, 2000.

JOURNAL AND/OR DISCUSSION QUESTIONS

1. What are three things you remember from this chapter?
2. Why do you suppose these three things stand out above all others?
3. What is comprehension, and what are the forms of memory?
4. What is the difference between hierarchical and reciprocal thinking?
5. What is the Cognitive Collective?
6. What is a major difference between thinking and feeling?
7. How does the IM and its components help with the teaching of thinking?

Chapter Three

Addressing Different Ways Through Assignments, Requirements, and Purposes

The Interactive Method's "different ways" approach to teaching and learning is in practice with this chapter's reference to (1) the assignment, (2) guides for creating and/or presenting/submitting for evaluation, and (3) purposes of the assignment. This author has used all or most of these tasks while teaching at varied grade levels throughout her career. When beginning her professorship at the doctoral, graduate, and then undergraduate level, lesson modeling was done with these assignments "adapted" to the curriculum for showing, in most cases, how to do the Interactive Method (IM) with respect to its components of the Interactive Book Report (IBR), Activity-Based Learning Center (ABLC), and Performance- and/or Project-Based Learning (P/PBL).

In the first book of this two book series, an interesting factoid is presented addressing how in 1998, this author's fifth-grade heterogeneous class made a 3½-foot-high and 20-foot-long IBR with Earth Day as the topic. That endeavor, with all students contributing one panel to the foldout IBR, won first place out of 600 entries in the NYS I'm a Green Nation competition.

Accompanying the assignments, requirements, and purposes, in one case, are the questions to be answered for a literacy history. And for the decision-making assignment, criteria, with excellence for meeting these, are given for the purpose of clarity. These projects and/or performances are designed for addressing the rationale of the IM by meeting objectives (see the first book's Chapter 11) and of goals for experiential teaching and learning, as presented in this chapter.

ASSIGNMENTS TO MEET OBJECTIVES FOR "DIFFERENT WAYS"

The first things to be addressed in the assignments that are forthcoming are that each one (1) involves the IM with (a) design and/or construction of instructional resource(s), and/or (b) recalling one's reading and writing history, (2) involves research conducted to produce an informational packet or brochure, and (3) a presentation or performance-type demonstration of the assignment.

It should be noted that for the college course, there are built-in portions of class meetings that include demonstration of the assignments with artifacts when necessary. Certainly, this could be applied to any class for any student at any grade level and is not exclusive to learners having different abilities or special ways.

For a college course, homework assignments usually address the reading of text from *Learning and Teaching Creative Cognition: The Interactive Book Report* (Schiering, 2015) and *Teaching Creative and Critical Thinking: An Interactive Workbook* (Schiering, 2016b). And homework is assigned at specific class sessions for discussion after journaling has been done by the teacher candidate outside of class.

The idea of this discussion is to bring forth not just the factual information addressed in the questions but a reaction to philosophies and research material conducted that's present in the textbooks. Comparison of opinions, whether in agreement or contrast to what is written, is believed to be important for intellectual exchange. The sequence of these assignments, aside from the first one, are not presented in a specified order.

The course assignments that follow are accomplished, at the college level, over a 26-session time span, with classes meeting for 2 hours and 10 minutes on Tuesday and Thursday. Some sessions have more than one assignment requirement due on the same date, depending on the allotted time for initial instruction and then presentation to the class.

As a teacher candidate or teacher, you are asked to please keep in mind, throughout this course or any class at any level, that we are a community of learners and educators. We are here to assist one another, practicing a positive manner and disposition. This is for the purpose of being most effective in teaching and learning for the ultimate benefit of those students we shall/do teach.

At the close of each presentation or demonstration of an interactive instructional resource, including any P/PBL assignment, the class members are called upon to (1) make statements that are positive based and (2) uplift the presenter by (3) acknowledging the work that was done to inform and enlighten the assemblage.

(A Cognitive Abilities Inventory, which addresses student learners' preferences for auditory, visual, tactile, or kinesthetic modality; room design; working alone or with others; structure or lack thereof; and other components of processing style, can be found online. The realization of preferences impacts relationships, honoring of differentiation of abilities and/or special needs, consideration of the influence of upbringing, brain hemisphericity, and neuroplasticity.)

1. Assignment: Sticky Hands: Getting Acquainted

Guides for Creating and Presenting or Submitting for Evaluation

A line is formed in the classroom and the leader walks around the room until the teacher/professor calls out "Sticky hands." At this juncture, each person is to find a partner and, raising their hands in the air, touch the fingertips of both hands. (There is hand sanitizer available for cleanliness before and after this exercise.) A conversation, as in talking "with" the partner, ensues. This conversation addresses such things as "home-type" topics of where one lives or would like to live, sports interests (as a participator or a viewer), family, friends, pets, vacation locations one has experienced or would like to go to at some time, and so forth. After a few minutes, the partnerships separate as "sticky hands two" is called out and people find new partners with whom to share.

Purposes of the Assignment

This is the first of three whole-class assignments for community building. This is a "getting acquainted" activity for gathering general information about class members. Ultimately, a connection may be made with respect to similarities and differences upon which to immediately reflect and have for future recall. The "sticky hands" activity is nonthreatening and promotes conversation with others, as opposed to "at" them or "to" one another. These "at" or "to" types of communication are formatted and done for dissemination of information as opposed to sharing, which is a "gluing agent" in communication techniques.

Additionally, there may be classroom discussions about building community within the school setting or classroom, which provide a means for preventing school violence, regardless of causes. The purpose is to share ideas for making our future classrooms a place where children enjoy the learning experience. Additionally, they are provided with the opportunity to be persons of good character, as well as implement a classroom rule of "No Put Downs . . . Only Lift-Ups!"

2. Assignment: Illustrated Folder

Guides for Creating and Presenting or Submitting for Evaluation

Using a pocket folder, the individual is to attach photocopied pictures, internet clippings, and/or typed material addressing the following on the outside flaps of the folder: interest areas; a few favorite book titles read to or by the individual; favorite quotations or sayings, especially that relate to literature and/or you as an individual; photos of friends and/or family; interest areas; and the like.

As you present, you may look down at your open folder and you "sweep" the class, which is seated in a semicircle. This way each class member gets to see your folder. As you present, use good voice modulation, point to illustrations or sayings, and read them when applicable. As a class member, you are to take notes on what was presented for future reference and conversations.

Purposes of Assignment

This is the second whole-class assignment for community building. The purpose of this introductory assignment is to establish a sense of togetherness. Similar to getting acquainted, but this time it is done with the folders providing permanency for later reflection. Questions regarding content material on the folder is anticipated for immediate reactions to sharing and purposeful showing of interest in classmates' work on this assignment. Discussion may follow regarding similarities and/or differences of material on folders' topics.

3. Assignment: Beliefs and Values Small-Group and Whole-Class Activity

Guides for Creating and Presenting or Submitting for Evaluation

The class leader explains and shows a slide for photographing or note taking that defines the terms *beliefs* and *values*. The class divides into groups and one person makes a list of the group's shared or envisioned beliefs and values.

Then, this scribe goes to the leader-provided chart paper with columns titled "Beliefs" and "Values" that is on the wall and transcribes the list their small group created. There may be repetitions of words in both columns. Historically, such repetitions have been (1) *education*, (2) *good health*, (3) *differentiation of instruction*, (4) *fairness*, (5) *kindness*, (6) *spirituality* or *religion*, and (6) *freedom*. An example of something valued but not necessarily believed in might be *chocolate*. What follows is a strong visual representation of the class's beliefs and values. Sharing is encouraged after the charts are read and the material on them analyzed.

Purposes of Assignment

This is the third whole-class assignment for community building. This classroom's small-group activity and sharing, followed by discussion, is done to realize what is believed in and valued from the class members' perspective/viewpoint. A sense of fellowship is, hopefully, forged. Customarily, similarities outweigh the differences. Cultural mores come to the foreground and an appreciation of differences in learning or what's valued is made clear during discourse of this topic.

4. Assignment: Your Personal Literacy History (LH) in Reading and Writing

Guides for Creating and Presenting or Submitting for Evaluation

Write a paper that traces your reading and writing history using the Literacy History Guide Questions. Then, bring the paper to class for sharing with a partner or two, depending on class enrollment being an even or odd number. Take notes on the similarities of your partner's LH to your own. Bring your notes back to class for whole-class sharing and discussion.

Purposes of this Assignment

The purpose of this assignment is initially for your examination of the influences your life experiences in these areas may have impacted your attitudes about reading and writing. It is believed that these attitudes will, in the long run, impact your future students with respect to the way you provide lessons. Additionally, since this assignment calls for classroom sharing, a viable means for comparing and contrasting literacy histories is apparent with the realization that as we are different, so are we the same; we share common social, societal, and academic realities.

Further Instruction for the L.H. Assignment

Your Personal Literacy History Questions

1. What were the first books read to you and what were the genres? Who did this reading?
2. When is the first time you recall reading on your own, and what was it you read?
3. What influence do you think this has on your present reading attitude?
4. Why do you suppose you selected particular books to read, and has this changed over the years?
5. What were your favorite books during ages 2 through 5, 6 through 8, 9 through 12, 13 through 18, young adult through the present time?
6. What type of reading was and is now done in your home by parents, siblings, relatives? Does this include newspapers and magazines? Do you presently read these forms of writing? Did you read these in the past? How do you think these have influenced you today?
7. How did reading in school influence you? How/did the reading habits of your friends impact you? Does this happen today? Why or why not?
8. Did you own a library card and/or go to the library to select books? At what age did this occur? Do you go to the library now? Why or why not?
9. What type of reading did you do in high school? What is your preferred genre of books presently?
10. Do you read for pleasure and if so, what?
11. Where is your favorite place to read for pleasure? How long has this been the case? Why do you suppose you prefer this location?
12. When is your preferred time of day for reading, and do you read silently or aloud? Explain your answer.
13. Do you like being read to at present? If not, when did reading aloud to you occur and end?
14. Do you read to others? If so, what type of book(s)?
15. What teacher, if any, had the greatest influence on your literacy history? How do you think this impacted your attitudes today?
16. What influence do you think your literacy history will have on the continuance of your reading as a learner and teacher?

Additional LH Commentary

Once these questions have been answered in a narrative format, there's a sharing of literacy histories to ascertain the similarities and differences in experiences and individuals' present attitudes. What this gleans for the learner and teacher is not just a comparison and contrast but a means for social literacy that creates classroom community. This is accomplished as one gets to know others' belief systems and the influences on their thinking and feeling.

This information impacts how assignments may be addressed by individuals, with negatives, should they exist, being examined for the promotion of success in the academic setting. For example, if one is not a reader and really dislikes reading, in the teaching situation, there is less of an interest to promote reading. The same goes for writing. However, if there's a love of reading and writing, or a like for one over the other, then the influence is perceived through the modeling of such attitudes, which impacts student learners. Knowing oneself as a reader and writer is incumbent on knowing how one came to his or her present disposition, which affects and has an effect on teaching dispositions.

5. Assignment: Decision-Making/Critical Thinking Graphic Organizer (DMGO)

Guides for Creating and Presenting or Submitting for Evaluation

The DMGO should have a title at the top with the word *problem* and the situation alongside that. Under this are three sections appearing from left to right with the words, *first choice*, *second choice*, and *another idea*. Or instead of *another idea*, put *third choice*. There should be at least three choices on this graphic organizer. Otherwise the idea of expanded thinking is not evident.

Under each of these choices, moving left to right, are the sections for "Possible Positive Outcomes" and then "Possible Negative Outcomes." There should be three possibilities for each choice in these "positives" and "negatives" areas. These are followed by the "Final Decision and Why," which is at the bottom of the foam-core board or poster board. (If this assignment is done on a computer, then the format is the same.)

Your final decision includes why you made that decision and *needs to contain information from the possible positive and negative outcomes you've written*. It would be an error to submit a reason not already addressed on the board. Follow the same pattern when orally presenting this graphic organizer to the class. The criteria for the highest level, 4, is described as follows:

Design: The overall look of the graphic organizer clearly showed the use of good color contrast. There was appropriate bordering and labeling when necessary. The flow, scope, and sequence were clear, with either lines or arrows showing the connection from one section to the other. The materials fit on the display board in the correct format style, as presented on the "examples" demonstrated and/or the handout given in class. The spacing of sections was such that the appearance of the graphic organizer was exemplary, as the font was large and easily readable.

Content: The "problem" was clearly stated, with a minimum of three choices. Each choice had three possible positive and three possible negative outcomes for the stated option. There was a "final decision, which clearly and exceptionally stated the reason(s) for that decision and the reason "why" was in one or several of the three sections under "Possible Positives" or "Possible Negatives." The scope and sequence were exemplary or quite good.

Grammar: The punctuation and sentence structure were completely correct.

Oral Presentation: The presentation demonstrated appropriate body stance, voice modulation, stress, and juncture, with good articulation. An interest in the topic was obvious, and the presenter was able to address questions concerning his or her final decision. This was clearly a demonstration of inductive or deductive reasoning. The presenter was affable and had a pleasant demeanor that connoted exceptional interest in the assignment presentation.

Purposes of this Assignment

At the onset, the purpose of this assignment is to have a realization of the steps taken for one to make a decision with the use of critical thinking (see Chapter 2 for Reciprocal Thinking Phases for cognitive and metacognitive skills applied regarding thinking skills in each phase). Candidates, through discussion and instruction, become aware that in most circumstances, only two options are usually presented for solving a problem. This either/or concept is replaced with the realization of there being more than two possible choices for problem-solving. There may be three or more possible choices, and this involves creative and concrete, as well as critical, thinking.

Another purpose of decision-making is how it's incorporated into the process of this assignment in children's literature, with the reader of a story examining, through reflection, the way a decision was made. Furthermore, analysis may be provided through classroom discussion regarding the critical thinking used for this story or for selecting a topic not in a book. The teacher candidates and future student learners benefit from seeing the process and then examining their own thinking as they prepare to make decisions. It's a practice that takes a lifetime to implement but begins here with steps involving cognitive awareness leading to self-actualization.

It should be noted that making a decision is an integral part of one's daily experience. This could be about deciding what to wear or which movie to see. As children develop their thinking skills, it is important to teach decision-making skills in preparation for use in later life situations. To have the skill of decision-making, one must first practice it.

6. Storytelling

Guides for Creating and Presenting or Submitting for Evaluation

This storytelling experience is clearly defined in the article you were given or appears at the end of this syllabus. However, for the purpose of this presentation, please be sure you are delivering your story *extemporaneously*.

You should use appropriate voice modulation, articulation, and convey interest while demonstrating an ability to answer and ask questions, which occurs following the telling of the story. Additionally, you are to have prepared your story in written format for the professor.

For the entire class and professor, you are to have filled in the Reciprocal Thinking Phases Identification Chart. Also, there are to be 10 convergent but mostly divergent questions and inductive and deductive reasoning that either extend the story theme and/or address the story using literal, applied, and implied comprehension questions. If asking a convergent question, follow it with why or why not or call for an explanation regarding the answer. These questions you design are not to be answered but are provided for class discussion and evaluation.

Remember that the overall idea, other than sharing the story, is for you to reflect and provide a means of reflective practice as well as comparing and contrasting empirical situations for your audience.

This assignment may also include a peer evaluation. Subsequently, a discussion may occur, in small-group format, following the telling of the story if time allows. The storyteller will inform the professor of the grade average he or she received after calculating the mean of the peer evaluation.

In summation, there are three parts for the entire class to experience and these are: telling the story, filling in the Reciprocal Thinking Phases Identification Chart, and extending the story through questions. And a fourth component of this assignment is submitting the written story to the professor, along with the Identification Chart and questions to extend the storyline.

Purposes of the Assignment

Aside from the idea of this being a means for creating classroom community and to exemplify social literacy, this assignment is designed to develop in you and later provide those you teach with these skills:

- Develop awareness of oral presentation style and public speaking
- Demonstrate scope and sequence in the storytelling format
- Prepare individuals for addressing what he or she is thinking and decisions that were made within the context of the story
- Analyze the thinking process through the completed Reciprocal Thinking Phases Identification Chart
- Synthesize the story events into a format that is structured chronologically or unstructured with flashbacks
- Provide the means for extending the story theme into different disciplines for the purpose of making the subject interdisciplinary
- Develop comprehension skills through designing questions that follow the filled in Reciprocal Thinking Chart, and subsequently provide application of cognition and metacognition skill-building. These questions should include ones that require inductive and deductive reasoning as well as convergent and divergent questions.

Another purpose of this assignment is to be aware of one's feelings and the difference between these and thoughts, ideas, opinions, and judgments. Subsequently, commonalities and differences within our shared environment are experienced for comparing and contrasting.

7. Assignment: The Interactive Book Report

Guides for Creating and Presenting or Submitting for Evaluation

The IM's IBR exemplifies project- and/or performance-based instruction, as learners work for reasonably long periods of time to research, investigate, imagine, and then respond to a question. This assignment involves creative cognition where you construct, using a binder and paper pages in page protectors, a book report addressing a piece of children's literature or a thematic unit of study. Each page involving the major disciplines of reading, language arts, science, social studies, and math need to be *self-corrective* interactive instructional resources (educational games, examples of which appear in Chapter 9) that you have designed and constructed. If self-correction isn't possible, then a sample of the completed discipline page needs to be provided. The IBR requirements include the following:

1. Outside cover page and inside title page, with the inside title page listing the name of the IBR's creator and for what grade this IBR is appropriate
2. Table of contents, with a listing of activities and the corresponding page on which each activity may be located (all pages that are in the IBR need to be numbered)
3. Author study, with the history of the author and the message of this piece of literature. If the IBR is on a thematic unit of study, select a storybook or informational book that addresses the topic of the IBR.
4. Reciprocal Thinking Identification Chart explaining what cognitive and metacognitive skills are addressed and developed when "playing the page" for each activity in the IBR. You may include Common Core Standards for each activity on the actual activity page.
5. Welcome page that invites students to play the pages
6. Designing a minimum of five (one for each major discipline of reading, English language arts, social studies, math, and science) self-corrective interactive instructional resource pages
7. Creative page ending the IBR. This page may be in any discipline of the five major ones or go into art, music, physical education, or careers

Purposes of the Assignment

The purposes of this assignment call attention to one's own thinking process, regardless of "what you are thinking." There is a stimulation of curiosity. There's a need-to-know driving component when creating and realizing how this activity works for information presentation and retention as well as construction of the interactive pages. Your use of creative cognition and critical thinking are major purposes as you design and create IBR pages. Inventing ways to stimulate students' interest through their active engagement in the IM processes are important by-products of this assignment.

Your personal use of imagination and creativity, whether linear or reciprocal, is incorporated into page design in the aforementioned disciplines. You may also address music, theater arts, and physical education as you develop pages for interaction. Role-play scenarios serve as a possible purpose of this IBR as you address social cognition through thoughts and feelings. Each activity allows for your development of using thinking skills to promote learning and retaining material through a hands-on approach.

Since the resources you make are self-corrective, you are fulfilling the purposes of causing you and/or your students to be self-reliant, empowered, imaginative, collaborative, disciplined, and engaging through communicating with one another as well as having the experience of "doing" this IM's project- and performance-based assignment.

The IBR is utilized as a prototype for future classroom use on a piece of literature or a thematic unit of study. Analysis, evaluation, comparison and contrast, classifying, prioritizing, decision-making (initial and advanced), as well as 18 other cognitive and/or metacognitive skills are used for investigation and critique when creating and later presenting the IBR.

A video-tape of your presentation may be made so that you may reflect on this presentation at a later date. The IBR addresses your creativity, use of your imagination, and overall, the *teaching of thinking*. Your exposure to and subsequent incorporation of learning standards from New York State and the Common Core Learning Standards (CCLS) and at all grade levels assists you in making connections between these and lesson goals. Standards, through designing, creating, and applying them, help you develop student learners' thinking skills, goal setting, and specifically, identification of critical and creative thinking skills.

Thinking wise, there is an ongoing review of the Cognitive Collective as one reacts and responds to the pages of the IBR. This reaction involves the examination of the pages, whether about the author, the story or topic, activity pages, and, before that, the welcoming page. There is an examination of design and color contrast, bordering, and inspirational sayings that are often woven into the IBR on the backs of pages.

Since this IBR involves you making a project, showing it, and having others play the pages, it serves as a classroom community builder. This is accomplished through the exchange of IBRs. Subsequently, students are teaching other students. There's a give and take or give and give in sharing what you know with others by using this instructional resource.

The final purposes of this assignment are designed to create a means of instruction that involve, engage, and address the utilization of a student's learning and processing style preferences. This is done while knowing which resources work for each student, thereby providing a classroom where the students are empowered and develop self-efficacy. Application and appreciation of one's creative cognition is also a key purpose.

8. Assignment for Teacher Candidates: Partnership Reading Lesson

Guides for Creating and Presenting or Submitting for Evaluation

This is a *three-part* assignment. First, you conduct research on an assigned reading method and create a booklet/packet containing this researched-based information. Then, along with the packet, a one-page trifold brochure is designed and created that has the key information about this reading strategy and is for classroom distribution. This is for later reference regarding personal use of information and review for future teaching situations.

Then, in role-play fashion, the teacher candidate(s) conduct a mock reading strategy presentation lesson. The key elements of the reading strategy are to be demonstrated so the class may see how this reading method is used in a classroom situation. The research-based packet and brochure that you have written is to be distributed to the class. Notes should be taken by those observing the reading lesson being demonstrated for their future reference. Teacher candidates may call on classmates to partake in the demonstration role-play of the reading method being addressed.

Purposes of the Assignment

A few of the initial purposes of this assignment are to demonstrate one's ability to conduct research, synthesize the information, demonstrate a selected reading method, and ultimately familiarize one's self and one's classmates with components of this particular reading method. Collaboration and addressing rules of engagements along with social literacy are continual purposes of this assignment.

When the reading method presentations are complete, the teacher candidates have at least eight different reading methods to examine and analyze for applicability in a classroom, along with how and when to use each of or some of these in that setting.

How to administer an Individual and Qualitative Reading Inventory is part of this research-based reading assignment. The purpose of knowing how to administer these is to make it evident as to where a student learner's reading problems may be present and why comprehension is impacted by one's reading ability. Additionally, when the reading methods presentations are complete, the class members are able to ascertain which reading method works best for specific reading problems.

The role-play demonstration lesson serves as a teaching performance. The reading method is demonstrated as if in a classroom setting. Subsequently, an additional purpose of this assignment includes practicing and then having the class observe the reading method for later comparison and contrast between actual reading or components of reading methods.

This demonstration lesson also serves the purpose of developing and applying *communication* techniques. This is accomplished as role-play lessons provide for classroom discussion focusing on *analysis* through *comparison and contrast* of these commonly utilized reading methods.

Note taking on a computer or by hand in class during the presentation allows for immediate and later feedback on what the individual considers of great importance in the demonstration. This form of written communication with one's self allows for deep analysis and introspective thinking as well as inductive and deductive reasoning. The creation of the research-based handout and the key elements of the reading single-page trifold brochure, when working with a partner, provided for continual collaboration regarding what is to be in these artifacts.

Notation

For a classroom, substitute reading methods with a topic of study that one might create a packet and brochure about and put on a performance/demonstration of key points of that topic. In a sixth-grade social studies class, an example would be addressing life in ancient Egypt, with a role-play of a day in that time period.

TEACHER CANDIDATES COMMENTS ON ASSIGNMENTS

These eight assignments have found teacher candidates providing six predominant reflections that have been repeatedly shared since 2000. These are paraphrased below:

1. One of the most important things I have as a "takeaway" from this class is that it's imperative for every teacher to have a respectful demeanor, regardless of where they are teaching. Depending on one's students to display that respectful demeanor is not the easiest of tasks. That is because some students respond quickly to a teacher when something is asked of them such as following behavior rules. They do this simply

because the teacher is the "authority" figure in the classroom setting. Also, they might respond because they were taught at home how to be respectful of others. Some students react very differently to teachers or to adults that ask them to comply with the codes of conduct that are in place (Spotkov, 2018).

2. A lot of times, a lack of student response is solely because they have never been asked to listen to someone and follow an instruction. It partially stems from what they were taught previously. If the students one is teaching are not respectful after they are told to be, they may have to learn how to be. This starts with the teacher, not making more rules but establishing relationships that will become the basis for respect and a caring and respectful classroom environment. Modeling respect, because I have it for myself, has to come before expecting it from others.

3. By doing the assignments, I gained practical experience for my classroom. I can see my students making an IBR with partnerships making pages for a unit of study. My partner and I did an IBR on a piece of literature. While I was making pages, I showed my family; they thought it was interesting while I was doing it, but when it was completed, they thought it was fantastic and a great way to learn. We gave the flip-chute to my cousin, who used it to study his multiplication tables, and guess what? He got 100 on the test. So the educational game resources my partner and I made were used in a practical way.

4. I think that true learning is not developed from sitting in a lecture and only listening. True learning comes by applying creative-thinking processes. There needs to be flexibility in the classroom and teacher open-mindedness when doing activities. There needs to be a nurturing experience, and this is what we had in our class. I really appreciated how our professor gave us many opportunities to provide feedback to our classmates after our activities had been presented. This motivated and involved us, and our confidence increased as well.

Teaching students to be creative by giving open-ended assignments that are project- and performance-based stimulates thinking and interactivity. This class provided a learning environment that continually involved giving ideas, presenting techniques, sharing talents, expressing opinions, inspiration, motivation, and collaboration. I learned so many great things from this class and cannot wait to incorporate what I have learned in my future classroom! (Gosken, 2018).

5. The storytelling was my absolute favorite assignment. Although I was nervous to present, it went well and everyone responded with positive comments. But just as importantly, we made questions to deepen the story topic and then discussed these and helped each other make good questions. The Reciprocal Thinking Chart was helpful, and I got to see how this helps teach us to think about what skills are being used. But the best part about the storytelling was that we got to know our classmates in a different way by hearing some experience from their life that made them who they are today. Some were really funny and some not like that at all. I discovered that we had a lot in common.

6. In other classes where we are working together, collaborating on projects could be difficult based on a student's lack of drive and motivation. When my partner and I worked on the IBR, we were uplifting and extremely positive toward one another and that led to success with reaching our goals. It's important to communicate and collaborate because it benefits the students. We used our creative cognition, and the hands-on work caused us to use our imaginations. At the end of the assignment, we both looked at each other like, "Wow, did we really just do this? Yes, we did" (Redondo, 2018).

JOURNAL AND/OR DISCUSSION QUESTIONS

1. How do the course assignments allow for the use of learners' imagination and creativity?
2. Which of the assignments do you think is most beneficial for creating classroom community, and why did you select that one?
3. How would you define the components of the IM?
4. What do you think are effective ways to involve students in their own learning?
5. What is meant by self-corrective work?

Part II

DIFFERENT LEARNERS = DIFFERENT WAYS: THE "HOW TO" OF THE IM

Chapter Four

Different Ways

Six Specific Types

This beginning chapter of Part II addresses different ways with use of the Interactive Method (IM) through students' learning by pace or ability level, kinds of instruction, interest areas, needs, and tier lessons. Any one of these may be applied to the narratives and examples found in Chapters 5 through 9. Additionally, in this chapter, an explanation is given regarding each of the aforementioned six types of differentiation. An example of this differentiation, applied in an instructional setting, follows each explanation of the differentiation type.

THOUGHTS FOR THIS CHAPTER

You're asked to remember that some students are stimulated by interest areas being addressed, others need more time to do work, and there are those who respond to certain kinds of instructions or have specific needs. Then, there are those who need structure and organization, and tier lessons work best for those individuals. Of course, there is the perceived ability level, but with the students working with the IM's self-corrective activity-based style of instruction, ability levels usually rise.

Interestingly, as college students at the undergraduate and graduate levels have told this author, after learning how to design, create, and make interactive instructional resources, they use the resources to teach themselves. And they simultaneously apply the type of differentiation (of the six types discussed in this chapter) that works for him or her.

SIX TYPES OF DIFFERENTIATION: EXPLANATION AND EXAMPLE

1. *Learning by Pace:* This involves the time on task that best accommodates a learner. While some students need a good deal of time to complete an assignment, others require less time or a small extension of time in order to address the material presented.
   Example: Writing examples of the four different types of sentences—declarative, interrogative, exclamatory, and imperative—has been assigned. Those learners who work at a slow pace will be allotted 20 minutes to complete this, while those who are able to complete work quickly or at a medium speed will be given 10 and 15 minutes, respectively.
2. *Learning by Ability Level:* This refers to the general expectation of student performance and competency at a given grade and/or age. Student learners may function at what has previously been determined as above, at, or below grade level. More specifically, achievement level may vary from one discipline to another so that grade or age level is acceptable, but content within a subject area may differ. Scores on standardized tests are often the determining factor for what is considered "on level" and what is above or below it.
   Example: The students have been assigned constructing an acrostic poem using a word associated with the summer season. Those who are adept at this would use a word like *summertime*. Those who are less adept would have a word of shorter length, such as *sunny*. Those with the least ability to construct an acrostic poem might be asked to use the word *sun*. The idea of using shorter words is to have the students working on level and feeling secure with the assignment, as opposed to working at a frustration level by using a word with a lot of letters.
3. *Kinds of Instruction:* This refers to instructional techniques or methods. Passive recipients of knowledge would be diametrically opposed to the instructional strategy where students are actively engaged in the process of acquiring information. The Socratic, Behaviorist, Experientialist, and Constructivist methods are a few of the ones practiced in schools and considered to be "kinds of instruction."

Learning through discussion, examples, types of questions, and inductive or deductive reasoning, as well as convergent and divergent questions and emotional components are considered when addressing this type of differentiation. Lessons are designed to be flexible; students work in collaborative groups or whole-class instruction with varied end products. Providing students choices as to how things will be done for the end product is another operative.

Example: The students have been assigned to conduct research on community helpers for later reporting to the class. Some would use the now popular internet medium to gather this information. Others might seek an interview with a community helper and take notes. Some might work passively and use their experiential past encounters or some television program with someone practicing this job to create an information sheet for later sharing.

Still others may watch a video that provides information or simply read the textbook and take notes on important points for information gathering and later reporting. Reporting styles would also vary in accordance with the kind of instruction to be utilized when disseminating information to peers as the final product for this differentiation.

For the final reporting, some students might prefer the use of PowerPoint slides to show what's been learned while others create an educational game. Some might want to create a puppet show with characters being community helpers. Or a role-play might be conducted with discourse between the community helper and another person or several other people. Those who favor lecturing might read their information to the class. Still others may ask students to contribute their experiences with community helpers to add to a presentation or create illustrations with commentary.

4. *Learner's Interests:* This refers to the areas where students are focused based on intentness, concern, curiosity, importance, consequence, and variations of thinking or feeling regarding learning fields. Some learners may want to gain information about sports, while others are not even mildly concerned with that subject.

Simultaneously, one may have curiosity about how to get from one place to another, while others are simply interested in someone else taking care of that arrangement. Interests are emotionally and/or cognitively based. They might involve using varied kinds of instruction, which corresponds to modality preferences, or they may involve construction of materials to facilitate students' learning.

Example: The teacher suggests that students create a chart to examine the similarities and differences between two characters in a selected piece of literature. Some students may be interested in creating a Venn diagram to illustrate these. Others may choose to conduct a mock interview, make an audio presentation, configure slides for viewing, make a mobile, conduct a scripted role-play, or use excerpts from the book's dialogue to show where the characters are in agreement or disagreement.

5. *Learner's Needs:* This is the subjective and/or objective evaluation component regarding instruction. While some students' needs are obvious, as in the hearing impaired student requiring an amplification system in the classroom, others are not as apparent. Student needs vary as much as individuals themselves at any given time. Emotional components, assessment tools, achievement in one area and not in another, students' sense of security, and stress factors are all considered when determining their needs.

Determining, through subjectivity, the needs of a student is feeling based. However, needs may be influenced by assessments, such as a response to intervention (RTI) or individualized education plan (IEP). Most importantly, learner's needs should be met by the teacher emphasizing a student's *areas of strength*.

Example: The teacher notes that several students in the classroom have hearing impairments. As a story is orally presented, these students may have a copy of the story to read silently. Visually impaired learners would have an audio of the story as backup. If a lesson focused on the use of writing notes where fine motor skills were employed and the students had difficulty with this requirement, the teacher might have assistance provided when these skills were addressed.

Emotional or special needs such as dyslexia, attention deficit hyperactivity disorder (ADHD), or decoding areas of difficulty would call for sand writing; structuring a lesson with notations on how the lesson is to be implemented, step-by-step; and using a whole-language approach for providing information or using guided reading techniques, respectively.

6. *Tier Lessons:* These are lessons where the assignment begins at a basic level and builds in complexity. The instruction is designed to add layers for greater cognitive skill application and comprehension. Tier lessons and/or scaffolding are implemented like the rungs of a ladder, where movement goes from lower to higher levels of understanding. Varying levels of achievement may be noted as students work in a small-group format for problem-solving and decision-making about the assignment.

Example: The teacher has assigned the construction of a three-dimensional flower for a classroom "garden." The students first discuss what it means to have something be three dimensional. Then, they decide on a type of flower they want to construct. Materials are gathered for this construction. The flower is put together with a means for having it stand freely. The flowers are put together to form a garden on a table in the back of the classroom.

DIFFERENT WAY SUMMATION: HETEROGENEOUS GROUPINGS

Regardless of the students in a classroom with respect to their different abilities or special needs or lack of either of these, there is most frequently heterogeneous groupings. This occurs in mainstream classrooms and classrooms that have communities of varied cultures or ethnicities. Some children progress faster than others while some do not and get labeled "slow."

The entire idea of the two books in this series is to use the IM and its components for the purpose of having instruction that involves the students in learning and engages these individuals and whole groups in learning that is attached to enjoyment of learning and retention of material. The six ways to differentiate may easily be part of each activity in the following Chapters 5 through 9. Knowing when to apply the differentiation relies on you, as the teacher, realizing the different abilities of your students and their personalities as well.

JOURNAL AND/OR DISCUSSION QUESTIONS

1. Which type of *different ways* differentiation do you prefer and why is that so for you?
2. How many of the six listed differentiations do you suppose your students would prefer?
3. How might you apply each of the *different ways* to a classroom learning situation when doing the IM?

Chapter Five

Twenty-Five Different Ways

The beginning of this book referenced the title for this part without emphasis on any specific way to educate. However, this chapter specifically addresses the concept of differentiation of instruction being synonymous or very similar to project- and performance-based work, as well as using the Interactive Method (IM) and the two techniques incorporating that methodology. Subsequently, this section has pages from teachers and former teacher candidates' Interactive Book Reports (IBRs) or Activity-Based Learning Centers (ABLCs) for examination and later application in your classroom for response to intervention (RTI) and/or individual education plans (IEPs). Or these resources may be a way of stimulating and utilizing creative, open-ended, and critical thinking.

A FABLE PROMOTING "DIFFERENT WAYS" FOR CLASSROOM INSTRUCTION

Before the instructional resources are presented, there is the 1940 fable by George H. Reavis, titled *The Animal School*. This piece seems to resonate with the idea of using "different ways/differentiated learning." His work is synthesized as follows:

An animal school was organized with an activity curriculum consisting of running, climbing, swimming, and flying. In order to make it easier to administer the curriculum, the school required that all the animals take all the subjects. What followed was chaos and disappointment for most, as the duck was excellent at swimming but was very poor at running.

The rabbit was excellent at running but suffered mentally when taking swimming. The squirrel was super at climbing but was frustrated with flying. The eagle was a problem child and was disciplined, as he wanted to do the classes his way. In climbing, he beat all others to the top of the tree but insisted on using his own method. The prairie dogs didn't go to school, but they would have if digging and burrowing, at which they were good, were added to the curriculum.

The moral of the story is that while there is a curriculum in which all may do well, not everyone does well with everything being done the same way at the same time. However, if that curriculum is expanded to involve interactive learning experiences, where all individuals may participate in accordance with their needs or abilities, then success is the normative result. With students' different abilities or special ways addressed, students' needs are met. When achievement is realized, the student result is empowerment, self-reliance, and willingness to move in the direction of continued learning with interest and, sometimes, teaching him- or herself. One thing's for sure: nothing ventured, nothing gained.

INTERACTIVE ACTIVITIES TO MAKE AND/OR PLAY

The pages that follow present ideas for in-class or out-of-school interactive differentiation of instruction in reading, math, social studies, English language arts, and science. Some of the activities involve drawing, cutting and pasting, inventing, constructing a figure, designing and making text structures/graphic organizers, role-playing, web quest interaction (technology), manipulation of index cards, making of activities by using ideas presented, following directions sequentially, and making puppets or geometrical shapes. You're invited to go forward and have fun!

Does It Melt?
Nicole Amato and Kristen Whitman

This activity involves identifying whether objects, when in the heat, melt or stay solid. Subsequently, this activity separates two forms of matter, solid and liquid. What stimulated this activity for class was that we read a piece of children's literature about crayons. We discovered, as a class, that crayons melt. A follow-up discussion about what melts and what doesn't took place. We decided to make a game of identifying what does and doesn't melt when exposed to heat.

Directions: Some picture cards of things that *melt* (dissolve or liquefy) and *don't melt* (stay solid) when exposed to heat have been cut out for you to copy, as shown in Figure 5.1. A game board has been provided, as seen in the same figure. See how the cards are classified into whether these pictured objects melt or do not melt. Next, we ask you to join in by either drawing small pictures of things that you think will melt or not melt, or get them from the internet. Clip art would be a good source for getting pictures.

Mount these drawings or pictures on cardstock paper. Cut them out and place the letter *M* (melts) or *S* (solid/doesn't melt) on the back of each card, depending on whether the object on the front dissolves or stays as a solid when exposed to heat. Then, separate the pictures as shown on the game board into "Melts/Liquid" or "Doesn't Melt/Solid."

Next, let others place the cards in what they think is the correct column. Answers can be checked by turning the card over and seeing what letter is on the back. Now you and those who play this game will be classifying objects, making an initial and an advanced decision, this will be as to what picture goes where, and self-actualizing when this activity is finished.

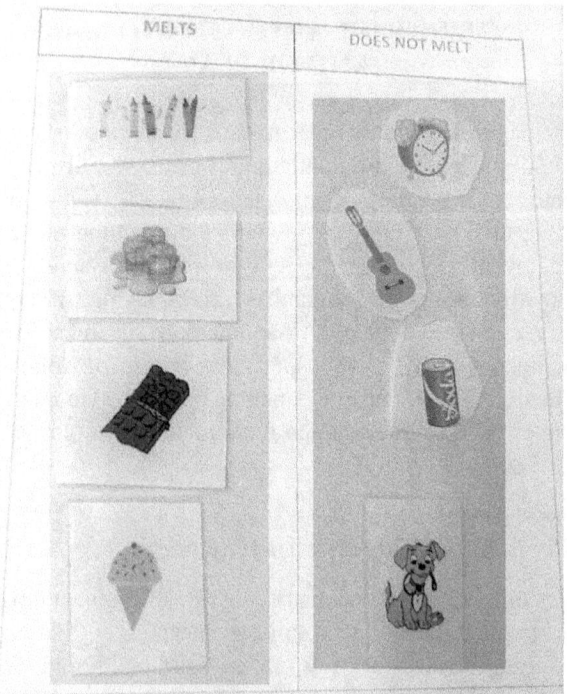

Figure 5.1. Does It Melt?

Number Line Challenge
Alyssa Wills

This activity provides a way for you to count backward using number lines. Also, there's solving subtraction problems. Different shapes may be used for the portions where numbers are to be placed. I used hearts, but you might use geometrical shapes such as squares, diamonds, rectangles, or triangles. Select a shape you'd like.

The main idea of this activity is to explore strategies to help you subtract while engaging your body in kinesthetic learning. Tactile involvement is a secondary modality as the numbers are placed on the number line. Hearing and seeing serve as the two other modalities involved, although to a lesser degree than the first two mentioned.

Materials: Number line taped on the floor from the largest number to the smallest. In this case, numbers 30–10; smartboard or whiteboard; fill-in number line (see Figure 5.2), subtraction problems on smartboard; dice; and answer key for subtraction problems.

Directions:

1. A number line, as shown in Figure 5.2, is teacher-made and taped in a semicircle on the floor. The numbers are to appear in each heart shape in sequential order. These numbers are cutouts and are to be taped inside the shape.
2. You stand behind a number in the line.
3. Starting at the largest number (30), you are to jump to the next number, counting back aloud while jumping until you are able to count back, independently, from 30 to 10.
4. The teacher or a classmate removes numbers from the number line and places these on the floor, inside the semicircle of the number line, as seen in Figure 5.2. The next thing to do is, working as a whole class, have one person at a time come forward, select a number from the floor, and tape it to the shape where it belongs in the line. This is done going from 30 to 10, or if counting forward, from 10 to 30. The check your work by making a guide sheet that has the numbers in order.
5. With the number line from the previous activity as a reference point, get a die and roll it. Whatever number is seen is to be subtracted from 30—example: 30 – 3.
6. Now, go to the number line, find the number 30, and count backward three numbers. This places you at number 27, which is the correct answer.
7. Suggestions: If you have the equation 25 – 7, then the person playing the game goes to the number line and counts back seven numbers from 25 for the answer of 18. Then, the player stands on that number. Addition, multiplication, and division equations may also be

Figure 5.2. Number Line Challenge

done, but the answers may not exceed 30, unless you increase the numbers represented on the number line.

Synonym and Antonym Match
Cynthia D'Antonio

Preactivities Exercises: In a preactivity lesson, the students have been discussing words that mean the same thing and also words that have opposite meanings. These are synonyms and antonyms, respectively. (A teacher-made list should be available that has easy and challenging synonyms and antonyms.) Students are to read the list to familiarize themselves with the words that mean the same or nearly the same thing and words that have different meanings.

Additionally, preactivity role-play may be done for some of the words on the list. An example of each might be demonstrated: synonym: happy–joyful; antonym: stop–go. Example demonstration: Synonym: A student comes into the room bouncing with joy to see everyone. The antonym role-play would be one person stands still and the other walks across the room. Of course, it's easier to role-play the antonyms.

Directions:

1. In whole-class format, make a word list of synonyms and then of antonyms. Be sure to have at least 15 of each.
2. Construct two 5-by-5-inch paper cutout hearts.
3. On one cutout, write (see Figure 5.3) "Synonyms: Same or Almost the Same Meaning," and on the other cutout, write "Antonyms: Opposite Meaning." Color these red, and tape them on the board for a board game or place them on the floor for a floor game. These will head two columns, one for synonyms and the other for antonyms.
4. Make one heart shape for each word on the synonym and antonym list (you should have a minimum of 30 words), and print one of those words on the heart shape. On the other side of the shape, put an *S* or *A* for *synonym* or *antonym*. This way, when the match is made, the students can self-correct.
5. Color these and, if possible, laminate the shapes. Each student selects a synonym or antonym and observes others' cards to find who has the card with almost the same meaning or an opposite one. Then, he or she places the shapes in the correct column.
6. Word Bank Suggestions: *Synonym Matches*: beautiful–pretty, cool–chilly, neat–clean, happy–joyful, break–smash, cut–slice, pick–choose, begin–start. *Antonym Matches*: awake–asleep, big–little, cold–hot, dark–light, empty–full, fast–slow, girl–boy, happy–sad, in–out, last–first, conceal–reveal, expand–contract, foolish–wise, horizontal–vertical, stop–go, up–down.

Wraparound Addition
Nicole Amato and Kaitlin Whitman

This is a self-corrective activity where you wrap a string around the cardstock paper crayon form to match it with the answer that solves the problem. Once you're finished, you can flip the crayon form over and see if your string matches the pattern on the back. If it does, you've done the problem correctly. If not, try again.

Materials: Construction paper, markers, string, imagination, scissors or hole punch.

Directions:

1. These construction directions appear in Chapter 9 under the heading of "Wraparound Directions." The first thing is to make a shape, such as a vertical rectangle (see Figure 9.9).
2. Punch half holes using a hole punch or make a cutout sideways *V* shape five times on the left and right side of the rectangle (or other shape). Put five equations on the left side and the five answers on the right side.

Figure 5.3. Synonyms and Antonyms

However, do *not* put the correct answer directly across from its equation.

Take a piece of yarn or string and tape it to the top of the rectangle. Starting from the back, put the yarn into the first open slot, and then wrap it around to the answer. Repeat this for slots/equations 2–5. Then, turn the rectangle over and underline the pattern the yarn/string makes. Unwrap the string and have someone do the activity and turn over the rectangle for self-correction. If the yarn doesn't follow the underlining on the opposite side, the equations and answers are not matched correctly.

Making a Sentence
Jordan Nadell

A whole class or several small groups can play this Making a Sentence game. It primarily involves the kinesthetic modality. The idea is for you to make sentences from a compiled list of 5-by-8-inch index card "word cards," consisting of nouns, pronouns, action verbs, and adjectives. The words are to be commonly used ones, such as words that are part of one's daily vocabulary. Engagement in the lesson with kinesthetic involvement is noted along with collaboration and cooperation of participants.

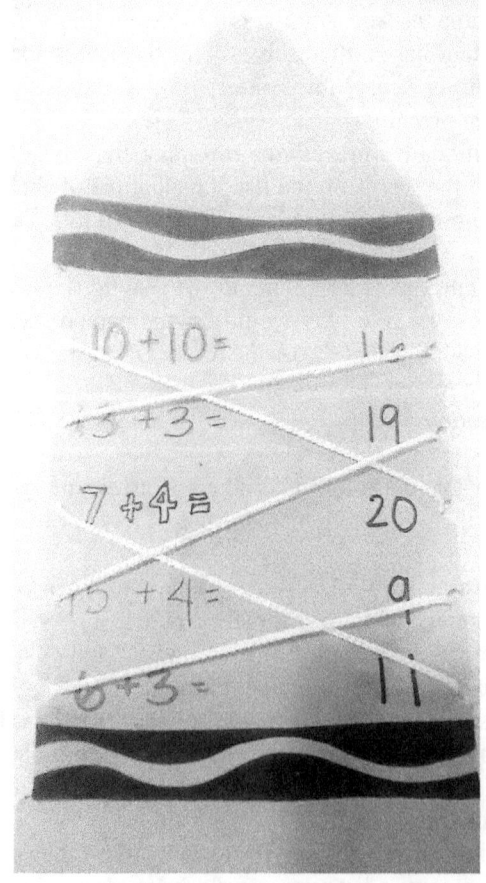

Figure 5.4. Wraparound Addition

Directions for Teachers:

1. Using index cards, make five each of the aforementioned parts of speech.
2. Put the word cards in a pile so each class member selects a word from one pile.
3. When all the students have picked a card, they will walk around the room talking to classmates and create a sentence by having at least one noun or pronoun to begin the sentence, an adjective, a noun, an action verb, and then a noun to complete the sentence.
4. The students then line up side by side to show the sentence that they made. "Sentence makers" are encouraged to make the sentence as long as possible with as many classmates participating as possible. (Although the cards in Figure 5.5 show words that begin with capital letters, it is suggested that lower case letters be available for sentence making.)

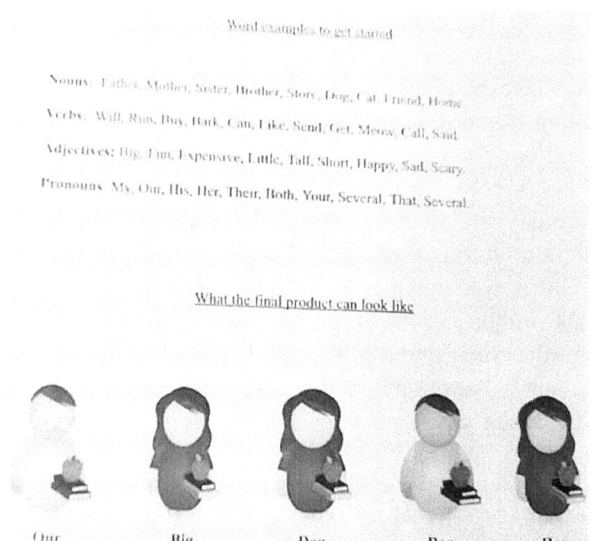

Figure 5.5. Making a Sentence

Tropical Rainforest Flip-Book
Kristen Dacunto and Meaghan Bosch

This activity is part of a thematic unit on the rainforest, as opposed to specifically being a page from an IBR on a piece of children's literature. The unit begins with the class watching a video about the different levels of the tropical rainforest. This is followed by a whole-class discussion, with handouts about animals that live in each section of the rainforest. With the use of several resources, such as the video, the internet, and a portion of the third-grade textbook, as well as *The Great Kapok Tree* by Lynne Cherry, the students are given instructions for making a Rainforest Flip-Book. *Materials:* Three different color sheets of construction paper, a stapler, markers, crayons or colored pencils, and a design in mind for decoration.

Directions:

1. Gather five different color sheets of construction paper.
2. Fold the first sheet down 4½ inches. Fold the second sheet 5 inches down. Fold the third sheet 6 inches down, and the fourth 6½ inches down.
3. Put one inside the other, with the top sheet's being the one that folds down 4½ inches.
4. Make a booklet and staple the top. Put decorative tape over the top, covering the staples.
5. Label each page of the flip-book as follows: (a) Tropical Rainforest, (b) Emergent Layer, (c) Canopy Layer, (d) Understory Layer, (e) Floor Layer.
6. Lift each flap, and, using information from what you've read or seen in the video and pictures, write about that layer. For example: The emergent layer is the uppermost layer with the most sunlight. Monkeys, birds, and butterflies live here.
7. Decorate the top part of the flip-book, and share this project with others in your class or another grade to help them learn about the rainforest.

Figure 5.6. Tropical Rainforest Flip-Book

Pumpkin Sorting: Small, Medium, Large
Nicole Lungaro

This activity is for an applied behavioral analysis (ABA) self-contained preschool class. The purpose of the interaction is for practice in sorting skills, grouping into three different-size groups.

Materials: Small, medium, and large pumpkins; paper sorting mats (see Figure 5.7).

Directions for Teachers: I taught this lesson to my class of three- to five-year-old preschool students. Our class is an ABA preschool class, consisting of seven spe-

Small   Medium   Large

Figure 5.7. Pumpkin Sorting

cial education students with a variety of learning abilities and challenges.

We first began by looking at the three sorting mats. Each was a different size, each was labeled with the words *small*, *medium*, and *large* in, appropriately, small, medium, and large print. The size of the lettering was used as a guide for students to see that letter size would match pumpkin size and help them sort these objects.

After looking at the mats, we brought them outside, where we found small, medium, and large pumpkins, earlier placed in the grass. Students were then asked to sort the pumpkins by size, placing the small-sized one on the mat labeled *small*, the medium-sized pumpkins on the mat labeled *medium*, and the large-sized pumpkins on the mat labeled *large*.

This getting of the pumpkins and putting them on the mat called for kinesthetic involvement for the students. Each preschooler helped others in the class and checked the size of the words on the mat while placing the pumpkins on the correct sorting mat. As a bonus to this exercise, counting of the pumpkins in each section was done aloud.

Math/Science Temperature Task Cards: Fahrenheit and Celsius
Janice Marmol and Barbara McMahon Egan

90 degrees is pretty hot
70 degrees is pleasing
50 degrees is getting cold
And 32 degrees is freezing

From our IBR on the unit addressing weather. We chose one activity for math that called for matching an illustrated "outside-temperature weather thermometer" with the corresponding "numbered" degrees. The idea of saying it is hot or cold outside becomes more definitive when one can read a thermometer and know the degrees of hot or cold. Knowing the temperature outside helps in everyday situations for choice of clothing or where one might go during the day.

If it is cold outside, let's say 20 degrees, then a 5-mile walk might not be a great idea unless dressed very warmly. Subsequently, as one discusses or learns about reading a thermometer, the topics of science come into play, along with social aspects regarding what activities

Figure 5.8. Math/Science Temperature Task Cards

are suited to particular weather conditions. One more thing this activity leads to is discussion about climate.

The main idea is to have the students read a thermometer and match that card, which has a thermometer and a red line showing the temperature, to the card with the corresponding number representing that temperature (see Figure 5.8). Temperature can be told in Fahrenheit (F) or Celsius (C).

Five-by-eight index cards were used and had a picture of a thermometer on one side and the temperature written in numbers on the other side. The cards were then laminated so they could be used many times over and cleaned with a sanitizing cloth. Next, each card was cut in half differently than each of the other cards. For example, one would be separated with a zigzag cut. Another card would be separated by a diagonal line.

The activity involved fine and gross motor skills/tactile modality. The cards were placed on the floor or a tabletop for matching. This is a self-corrective activity because it's a shape match. The color of the font and printing style are the same, as are the cards, so only the shape makes the match when fitting the cards together. Each of the thermometer cards have Celsius or Fahrenheit on the bottom of it. You are asked to make a set of cards to help students learn how to read a thermometer and know the outside temperature by reading the degrees on the thermometer.

Cloud Making
Barbara McMahon Egan and Janice Marmol

Directions: There are many different types of clouds, but only three have been selected for illustration in this activity. The supplies you'll need include cotton balls, glue, scissors, a piece of dark-color construction paper to represent the sky, and yellow construction paper to use for making the sun.

The dark-color construction paper is already labeled with the name of the cloud and a short description of each cloud, which will help with our design. If you get stuck on a specific cloud design, use the model in Figure 5.9. Use your imagination and create beautiful clouds. The sky is the limit.

Under-Over Sewing
Jennie Moore

Fine motor skills can be fun to practice. See the sewing cards in Figure 5.10. Trace them and then enlarge them if necessary. Color these cards of an owl, bear, fox,

Figure 5.9. Three Cloud Types

frog, and hedgehog using bright colors and good color contrast. Punch holes with a one-hole punch and gather up some yarn. Put the yarn through the first hole from underneath the card. Then, go over to the next hole and go under to the next, going under-over until you're done with the sewing. For fun, you can go backward and do over-under sewing.

Sequence of Events Story Train
Steven Malinowski and Tyler Cox

There are many events that take place in the story *Oh, The Places You'll Go* by Dr. Seuss. For this activity, we've selected the three sequence words of *beginning*, *middle*, and *end*. Other sequence words can be used for things like the life cycle of an animal or a made-up story about going on a vacation, to a friend's house, the zoo, a playground, and so on. These sequence of events words would include some of the following: *first*, *next*, *then*, *before that*, *after that*, *now*, *yesterday*, *today*, *tomorrow*, *in the future*, *second*, *third*, and so on. When you make your sequence activity, you might use other shapes instead of a train.

Figure 5.10. Under-Over Sewing

Directions:

1. Make a drawing of a train or get one on the internet, print it, and cut it out. Be sure to have at least three train cars for this activity.
2. Cut out circles using brown or grey construction paper and put a smaller and lighter circle inside that first one.
3. Use a triangle and a half circle to make the front part of the train. The smoke stack is a rectangle with an upside down hexagon on top of it, and three circle shapes coming from the smokestack to represent this being a steam engine. All shapes are made from construction paper or may be printed from clip art on one's computer and glued to heavier paper such as cardstock or poster board.
4. Put the train together, and use white construction paper for engine windows in square and rectangular shapes.
5. Using different color paper with white inserts, write the event and then an illustration from the book that can be drawn or photocopied to help identify the setting of the explained event. On the back of each sequence card, put a number from 1 to 9 (depending on how many events you have) for verification of sequence.
6. Put the train in order and place the train on the floor with the sequence cards randomly arranged on a tabletop or floor. Arrange the cards on the train in the order that they happened in the story.

Figure 5.11. Sequence of Events Story Train

Color-Mixing Electro-Board
Kaitlin Whitman and Nicole Amato

There are so many colors! Some colors are called *primary colors* and these are red, yellow, and blue. Secondary colors can be made by mixing two primary colors together and they form the secondary colors of orange, green, and violet. This activity involves mixing primary colors to make secondary colors and then, in two cases, using a primary color with white to make a new color. You'll be using an electro-board for the parts with color and a continuity tester to see if your answers are correct.

The directions for making the electro-board are in Chapter 9, Figure 9.10. When you go to test your answer for correctness, you'll need to place one finger of your left hand on the brass fastener on the left side of the "board" and holding the tester in your right hand, put it on what you think is the answer. If the light lights up, you are correct and if it doesn't, then try again. This is a self-corrective activity involving mostly the tactile and visual modalities. Let's see what color combinations are made when mixing them together!

Know Your Weather
Tyler Cox and Steven Malinowski

You're familiar with task cards from Figure 5.8. So you know how they work with respect to matching-by-shape puzzle pieces you make yourself. This set is one we constructed regarding different types of weather. Each card

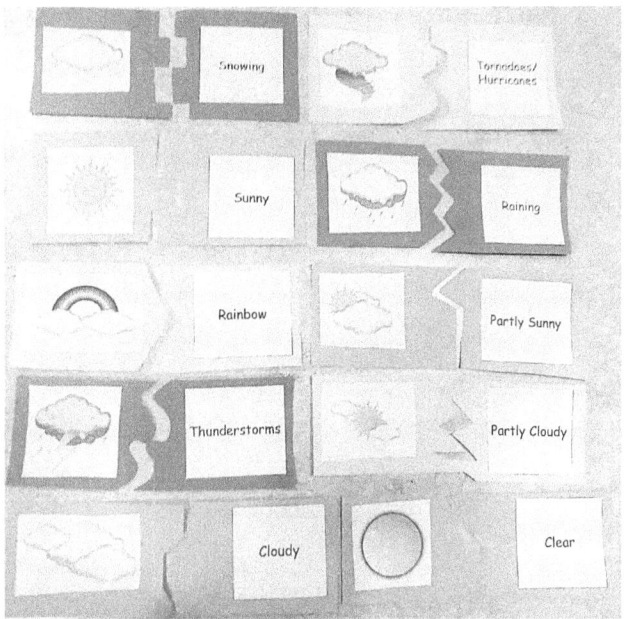

Figure 5.13. Know Your Weather

has a picture on one side and on the other is the name of that type of weather. This may be considered an early identification, primarily tactile game for primary-level learners. See the illustration in Figure 5.13 and make some "weather" cards with pictures and the words that name the weather type. Have fun!

Addition Number Picture Puzzle
Alexis Correa and Emma Kaiser

This activity is a left-side, right-side puzzle match. It could be done as a top or bottom match as well. For this game, half of a 5-by-8-inch index card is cut in half *horizontally*. On the left is an addition equation; however, depending on grade level, it could be subtraction, multiplication, division, ratios, equivalents, or a myriad of other math problems. Word problems easily could be used for this mainly tactile and visual game. An example of a math word problem would be having on the left side, "Tom had seven (7) red apples and five (5) green ones. How many apples did Tom have in all?" On the right side of the card, you'd have the answer number be 12. An illustration of 12 apples could also be present for a pictorial view of the answer.

Directions: Find the math equation cards and line them up one under the other. Next, in the mixed-up picture and number answer cards, find the card that answers the equation. When you're done, simply mix up the cards again or make new cards and share the game with classmates. Depending on the math function, this game could be used for different abilities or special needs from preschool through upper grade levels. The idea is the students are actively involved in their learning.

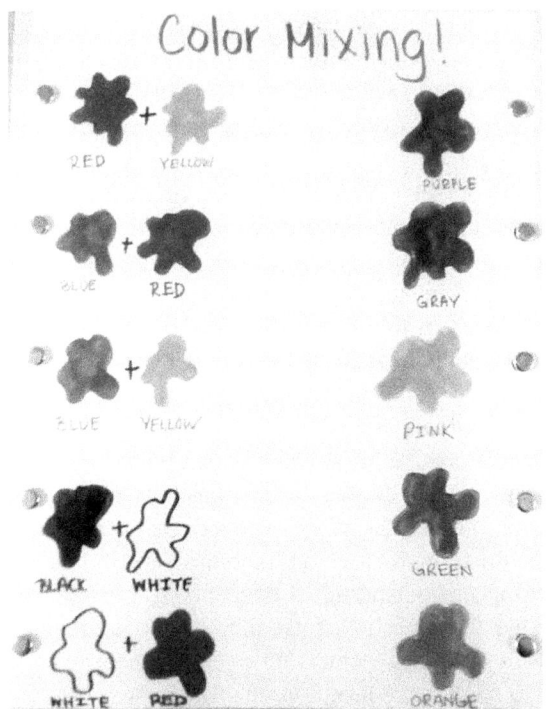

Figure 5.12. Color-Mixing Electro-Board

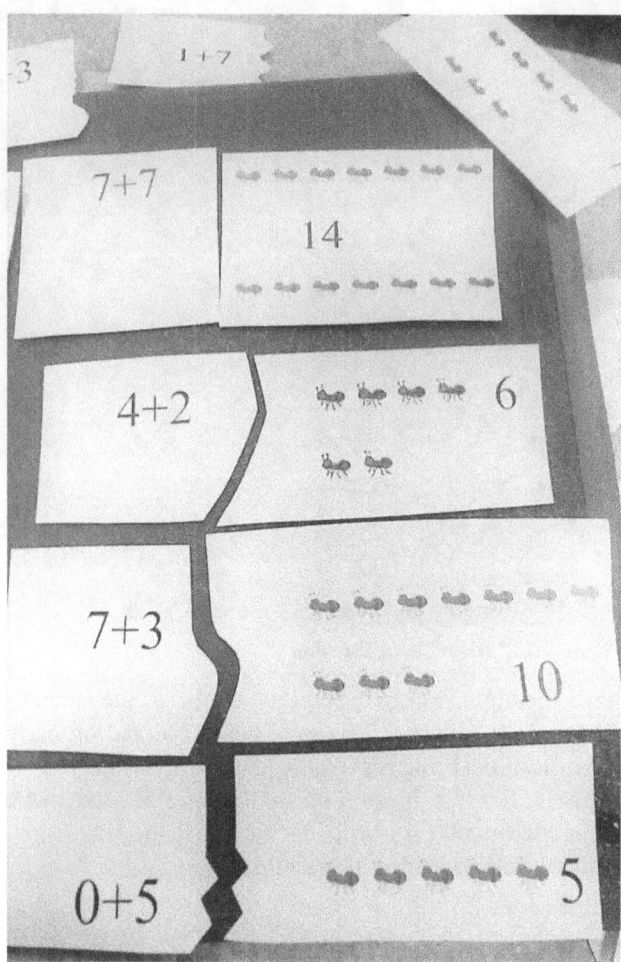

Figure 5.14. Addition Number Picture Puzzle

Figure 5.15. Life Cycle of a Frog

Life Cycle of a Frog
Meaghan Bosch and Kristen Dacunto

Wrap the string around the card stock paper from left to right to match the model frogs to the description of each stage of its life cycle. This three-dimensional wraparound gives the students an opportunity to touch the figures to feel the shape of them while verifying the stages and general size of the stages of the frog's development. This hands-on activity is for early level learners or even preschool children.

Puzzle Tower Our Way to Learning! Using Jenga for Higher or Lower Order Thinking
Madeline Craig

Game Overview: Jenga is a traditional game of block restacking while attempting to avoid having the tower collapse. The game originated in the 1980s and contains 54 blocks that need to be removed one block at a time and then placed on top of the tower. This creates an unstable structure that must be carefully navigated by each player.

There are many examples posted on the internet of using Jenga for other purposes aside from its original entertainment intent. Most of these examples include people writing their own questions on the game pieces and the game play involves answering the questions one by one until the game tower falls. The questions can be a way to get to know one another or to offer dares to complete certain challenges or to learn a particular subject content.

Creating the Game: The first step would be to purchase a Jenga-type puzzle game (of if you are handy, make it yourself). You can buy the original Jenga board game or any of the generic versions of this block game. I found a generic one at a popular department store and used a label maker to put key concepts from the unit on most blocks in the game. In order to use the game for multiple content areas, I used a permanent marker to write key concepts on the other side of each of the blocks that were already labeled with a concept.

Then, I created an associated pamphlet that asks students to answer higher order questions about the key concept. You could, if you wanted, just ask students to define the terms written on the blocks and in this way be checking understanding of concepts at a lower level of thinking. The questions I ask in the pamphlet require students to make connections between concepts and explain how to apply the concept in the classroom.

How to Play the Game: It is important to explain and demonstrate the game carefully to students so they understand the goal of the activity, learning outcome(s), and how it will help them learn the course content and, if possible, link it to real-world application. In my case, I explain to the students that it is necessary for them to know and be able to apply the key concepts of the unit for their teacher certification requirements as well as in their own classrooms in the future.

Players proceed one by one, removing a block from the tower using only one hand at a time and then carefully stacking it on top of the tower to avoid tower collapse. The person who makes the tower collapse traditionally loses, but below are different ways to play the game in groups with various outcomes.

1. Competitive Falling Play—Groups try to compete against each other to have their puzzle tower last longer than the other groups. The last group whose tower does *not* fall wins the game.
2. Competitive Pamphlet Play—Groups try to compete against each other to complete the most questions in the pamphlet before their tower falls.
3. Noncompetitive Play—Groups are tasked with completing all aspects of the pamphlet regardless of whether their tower falls during play or not.

The use of the pamphlet drives this activity to a higher level of thinking. If students are asked to pull out blocks from the tower and simply define the term labeled on the block, they would be achieving a lower level of thinking, such as understanding. Completing the pamphlet requires further thought and explanation of the key concepts and their real-world application in the classroom. In many cases, this would require groups to (1) perform some research on their devices or (2) in the textbook or (3) use articles posted in the learning management system to apply the key concept. A simple block-stacking game can, therefore, be used to differentiate learning for a variety of learners.

(To make the game applicable for lower grade-level students, you would select a topic in the curriculum for the questions. This could be knowing a part of speech, with the blocks having different nouns, verbs, and adjectives on them. Or the blocks could have multiplication equations on them to be answered. The beauty of this game is that it may be modified for a number of topics and/or different ways applicable for a designated grade-level curriculum.)

Figure 5.16. Puzzle Tower Our Way to Learning

The Future You!
Tyler Cox and Steven Malinowski

In the Dr. Seuss book *Oh, The Places You'll Go*, Dr. Seuss refers to the places we travel, emotionally, from childhood through later years. In each stage of one's life, he remarks that we'll be in places we don't like or ones that we favor over others. Regardless, his overall message is that we'll move forward and be successful.

We say that you never know, when looking to the future "you," where you'll be or what you'll be doing. But you can have aspirations or goals. Let your imagination kick in for this activity! We selected a "hot air balloon" illustration, as it's going up, in Figure 5.17 in which to draw a picture of what you want to be when you're older. Then, write a few sentences about this illustration.

Calendar Creation
Janice Marmol and Barbara McMahon Egan

What do you think of when someone says it is spring, summer, fall, or winter? We think of what the weather is like, the temperature outside, the months associated with that season, clothing people wear, and activities that go on during that time of year. So we decided to make a calendar with those categories and hope you'll join in and do the same! We also made cutouts of things in the different categories mentioned. The final calendar is seen in Figure 5.18. Here's how to make one of your own.

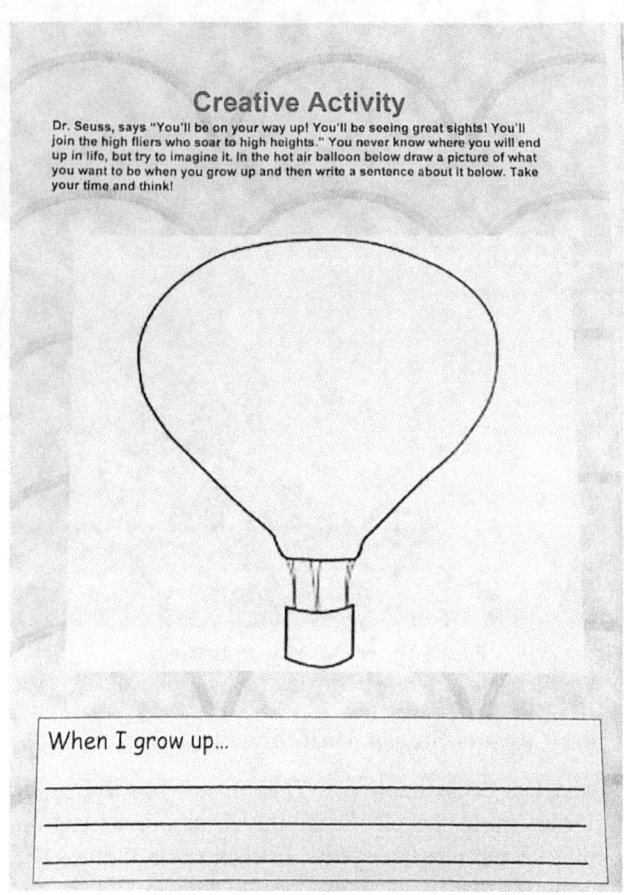

Materials: One 8-by-11½-inch piece of cardstock paper in white or a light color, markers, ruler, pen or pencil, color pencils, and internet clip art.

This is an individual, small-group, or partnership project! You decide.

Directions:

1. Using the cardstock paper, divide it using a ruler and making ink lines, with five sections going down and six sections going across.
2. Going vertically and horizontally, label the sections. On the left side write: Season, Spring, Summer, Fall, Winter. Across the top, after the word *season*, going from left to right, write: Temperature, Month, Describe Weather, What Do You Wear?, and What Activities Can Be Done?
3. Using the computer's clip art or your drawings, have illustrations of the temperature, months, weather conditions, clothing worn, and activities one might experience in accordance with each season.
4. Put these, using poster putty, in the sections that correspond to the category. A filled-in calendar is seen in Figure 5.18. Feel free to come up with ideas of your own for any of the categories. Please share your designed and created calendar with classmates.

Figure 5.17. The Future You!

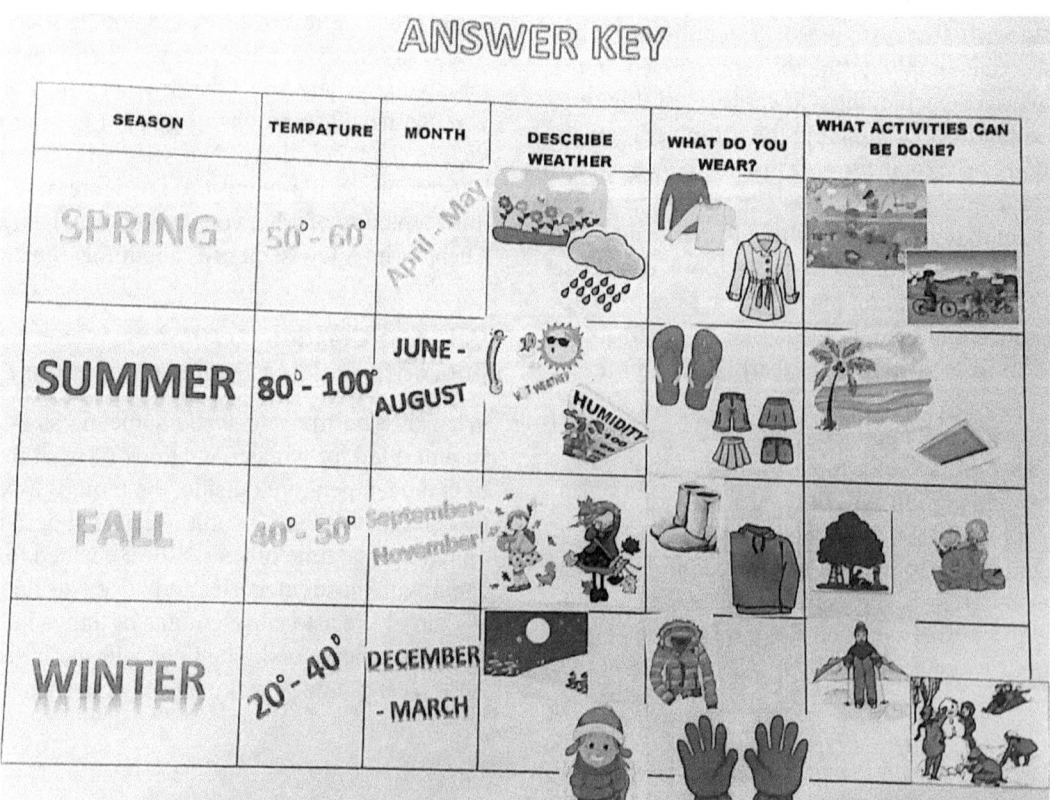

Figure 5.18. Calendar Creation

Character Captions
Ilyssa Polirer and Catie Mae Rocioppi

This is a total kinesthetic modality floor game! We read the book about Junie B. Jones in Hawaii. The author, Barbara Park, described the characters very well so the reader could know them, as if he or she were there in the story. So we made a floor game with pictures of story characters and what Junie B. would say about each picture.

The interesting thing is that after we made the game, we thought this would be good for class pictures and putting the pictures on a bulletin board and writing captions for them. Some could be silly if we had a funny pose, others could just be what's happening in the picture or who's in it. Or get some family pictures and make a photo album with captions or a floor game of your own with pictures of vacations, favorite places to go, or foods liked. The idea is to have an illustration and caption it.

Materials: Shower curtain liner; dark colored markers; pictures of persons, places, or things; and different color construction paper; 3-by-5-inch or 5-by-8-inch index cards; Velcro tabs.

Directions:

1. Choose your topic for the floor game pictures and then gather at least 10 pictures. These may be photograms or pictures you draw or photocopied from a book. Also have a shower curtain liner on the floor.
2. Mount the 10 pictures on a piece of colored construction paper that contrasts with the shower curtain liner. Make sure the outline shape of the picture is not too wide.
3. Be imaginative when you then write captions for each picture on a 3-by-5-inch or 5-by-8-inch blank index card.
4. Velcro tab the shower curtain liner and back of the picture card.
5. Place the captions next to the pictures and enjoy the read with classmates.

Figure 5.19. Character Captions

Moon Phases Find
Danielle Valente and Kaitlin LaCasse

This activity is an electro-board; directions are given in Chapter 9, Figure 9.10. This activity is self-corrective and addresses the phases of our moon. There are waxing and waning crescent and gibbous shapes as well as first and last quarter and the full/new moon. Using the continuity tester, see if you can match the name of the phase with its shape.

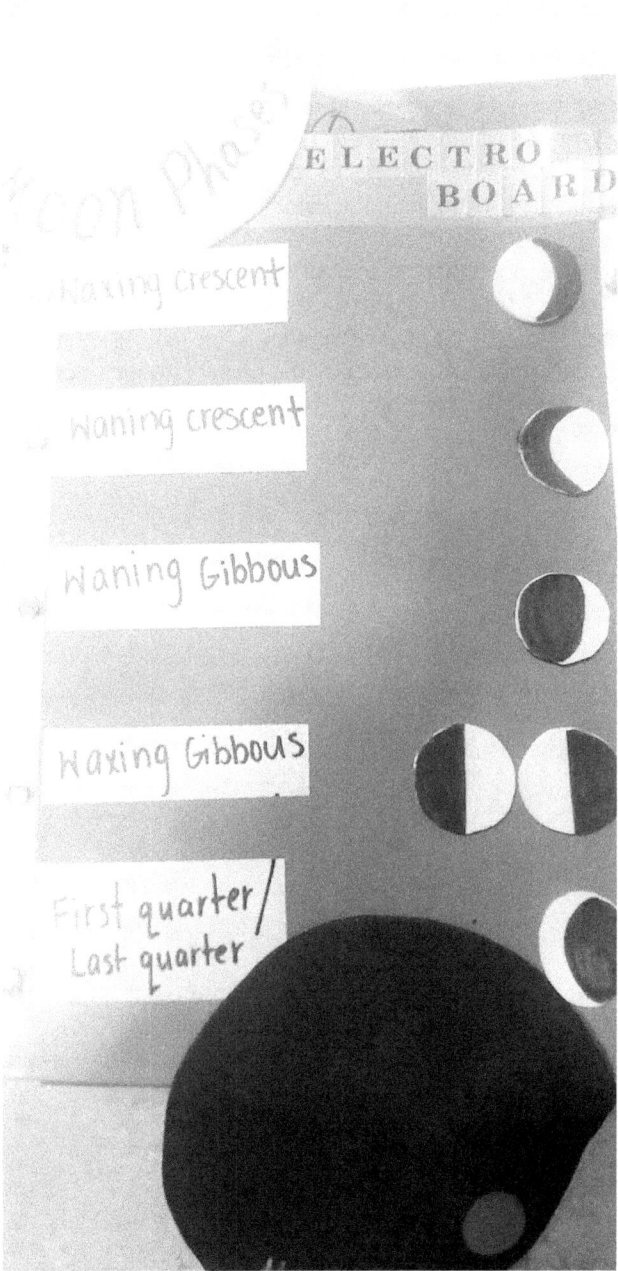

Figure 5.20. Moon Phases Find

Who Am I: Guess the Planet
Kaitlin Lacasse and Danielle Valente

This game gets you to learn interesting facts about the planets in our solar system. The object of this game is to go through the fact boards/pieces and identify the planets in our solar system by identifying their characteristics.

Materials: Book or internet to get facts about planets, poster board cutout pieces 4 inches wide by 8 inches top to bottom, markers and light color construction paper cut in rectangles that are 3 inches wide by 1½ inches high.

Directions: Cut out the poster board (or cardstock or foam) pieces so that they measure 4 by 8 inches; have these in a dark color so there will be color contrast with the rectangular light cardstock pieces measuring 3 by 1½ inches. Using a reliable resource, gather three facts about each planet. Put one fact on each rectangular piece and then glue that piece to the dark-color board. The last "Who Am I" piece should fold in half. Lift the fold upward and write the name of the planet there so that when someone lifts the flap, the name of the planet is revealed.

To help you recall the order of the planets, try this acrostic poem **My** (Mercury) **Very** (Venus) **Enlightened** (Earth) **Monkey** (Mars) **Just** (Jupiter) **Sat** (Saturn) **Under** (Uranus) **Napkins** (Neptune). Put the "Who Am I" boards in the same order as the planets in our solar system for self-correction.

Fun With Tallying and Graphing
Margaret Paccione

When we started the data collection and graphs chapter in our math textbook, the students learned about tally marks, graph keys, bar graphs, picture graphs, and line plots. As a culminating project and a chance for collaborative group work, the students worked in groups of three to four to create a survey, ask students in other classes to participate in their survey, and create a graph to record the results. It's a great opportunity for students to practice their collaboration and communication skills.

Materials: Paper, pencils, and crayons or fine-tip markers.

Directions: Separate the class into small groups and distribute a survey packet. This contains Data Collection and Analysis, Survey Question Sheet, Data Collection Results, and My Group Work Evaluation, as shown later in this narrative.

After putting the students into groups, they are given the Survey Question Sheet. The first step is for everyone in the group to come up with *one* idea for a survey—for example, favorite movie or sport, clothing type, foods, and so on. Group members record the ideas of their group and decide which idea they are going to tally and graph. Some students like to give reasons for their choices and try to convince their group members their choice was best. Other groups like to decide by having a vote.

The next step for the students is to decide what type of graph to create. Their choices are a bar graph or a picture graph. In the interest of time, I recommend a bar graph. Then, the students decide what job they will have when taking the survey and what color they are going to choose to color in the graph. After the packet is completed, the students go to another classroom in the school to gather the data for their survey. I always make sure to speak with the teachers beforehand to set up a date and time that is convenient for my students to come in and take a survey.

When conducting the survey is complete, each student reads their "part" and they all record the results on their Data Collection sheet. They come back to class and begin working on their graph. As I observe the students working, I observe how the students are communicating with each other and whether they are staying on task. I make note of any conflicts that arise. If a conflict does occur, I determine if it can be solved within the group or if teacher intervention is necessary. I take notes of things I hear the students say—both positive and negative.

Once their graph is complete, the students fill out a Group Work Evaluation. It's a helpful tool, because I can compare these with my notes. In addition, I have hard data to use to make adjustments to future groups. Finally, I can differentiate activities to give students additional opportunities they might need to strengthen their collaboration and/or communication skills.

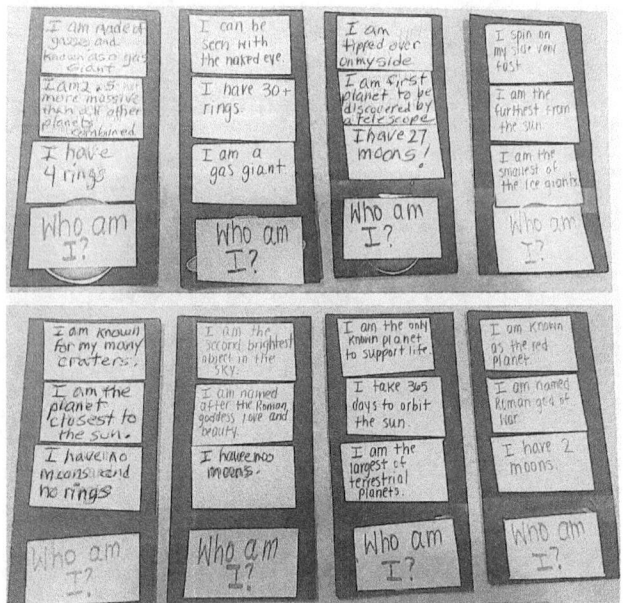

Figure 5.21. Who Am I: Guess the Planet

Name_____

Data Collection and Analysis

1. Discuss with your group the types of "survey" questions you would like to ask. For example, favorite sport, favorite ice cream, favorite color. Write the ideas on the lines. Each person should share one idea.

    My Idea _____
    My Partners' Ideas _____ _____ _____

2. Talk with your group about which *survey* you would like to *complete*. When you have agreed on the idea for the survey, write it on the line. _____
3. Talk with your group members and decide what type of survey you would like to *create*: bar graph or picture graph. Write the type of graph you will be making on the line. _____
4. Talk to your group about the job that you would like. When everyone agrees on the job they will do, write each group member's name next to their jobs.

    Introducer _____
    Survey Question Reader _____
    Choice #1 and #2 Reader _____
    Choice #3 and #4 Reader_____

5. Fill out the question sheet for your survey. When you have finished, write "Done" and put a smiley face on the line. _____
6. Visit the class you are going to survey. Make sure you use tally marks to collect your data!
7. Pick up your graph paper from the teacher and find a quiet place in the classroom to work with your group. Remember to ask your group members if you have a question. Also remember to give your group members compliments and offer to help!

Survey Question Sheet

You will be taking a survey in another class. Make sure to fill in the Survey Sheet and write everyone's name down next to their part.

REMEMBER TO USE TALLY MARKS TO RECORD YOUR ANSWERS!!!

   Introducer _____ My name is _____.
   Survey Question Reader _____ We are taking a survey about_____
   Choices Reader _____
   The choices are _____, _____, _____, and _____.
   The Data Reader will read the choices one at a time. Record the results on the Data Collection page.
   Data Reader's Name: _____

Data Collection Results

   Choice 1 _____   Tally Marks _____
   Choice 2 _____   Tally Marks _____
   Choice 3 _____   Tally Marks _____
   Choice 4 _____   Tally Marks _____

My Group Work Evaluation

Name_____ Date_____

Group Members' Names_____

Think about how you worked with the people in your group today. Then, decide which answer best describes how your team worked together. Next, fill in responses to the statements on the bottom of the page with *personal comments*. These read (1) My group finished on time and we did a good job on our project; (2) I helped others and cooperated with my group members; (3) I listened to my group members' ideas; (4) I used my indoor voice when talking with our group; (5) We did best at . . . ; (6) Next time we may try working more on . . . Full statements or one of these three "faces" may be used to address items 1–6:

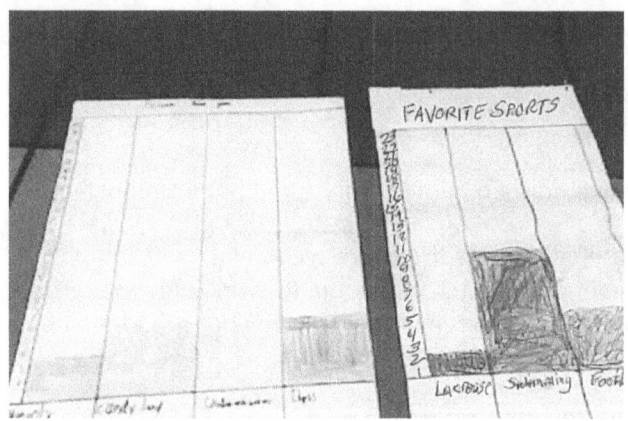

Figure 5.22. Fun With Tallying and Graphing

Character Heads-Up
Michelle Cronolly and Steven Lessin

We used the children's literature book *Charlie and the Chocolate Factory* by Roald Dahl. However, any piece of literature could be used for this activity, at any ability. If you're doing a thematic unit on a topic such as pioneers, solar systems, community helpers, or varied math functions, geometrical shapes, food groups, types of storms, butterflies, historical events/figures, just check your curriculum, this activity is adaptable.

Students, using their role-playing skills, imagination, and knowledge of either the main character or topic, see how well they know the story characters or unit of study. This is a partnership, small-group, or whole-class activity. The literature piece or topic will determine how many headbands are made—one for each character or portion of the topic. We used the aforementioned book and had six characters represented (see Figure 5.23).

Materials: Construction paper, colored pencils, color markers, charter photocopy or drawn picture cards, at least 5 blank index cards, and Velcro tabs.

Directions: Using construction paper, make a headband for each character in the story or section of the topic to be addressed. If, for example, you're doing a unit on weather and are addressing storms, you'd have at least five headbands. Next, working in small-group format, make a drawing of each character in the book on 5-by-6-inch or smaller blank index card. If the thematic unit is on community helpers, you'd have six or seven of these headbands or drawings. Storm types would require five drawings or cutouts. Put a Velcro tab on the center of the forehead part of the headband and on the back of the picture card.

Have one student, with eyes closed, select a picture card from the cards and another person attach that card to his or her headband. Once the character card is attached to the headband, the person can open his or her eyes. One or a few people can role-play, for the person wearing the character card, how that character acted or things that character said in the story. The student wearing the headband character card guesses who the character on the headband is. Once a correct guess is made, repeat the former steps with a new character.

Now, if you're doing community helpers, the role-play or dialogue is done the same way as the aforementioned, and that applies to most topics. Be sure to be creative in your portrayal of persons or events.

Three-Dimensional Super Word Search: Geo-Board
Joann Larkin

This is a new way to do a word search because it's very different than the pencil-and-paper, circle-the-word type you're accustomed to doing. This one requires using your tactile modality a lot. Here's how it works, as seen in Figure 5.24:

Figure 5.23. Character Heads-Up

Materials: A wooden or foam-core board, rubber bands, word search template, small nails or push pins.

Directions:

1. If you're making a wooden-base word search, you first need an 8-by-11-inch piece of wood that is thick enough to hold small nails being hammered into it.
2. Hammer in the small nails 14 across and 14 down on the board. This means you'll have 196 nails hammered into the board.
3. Create a list of words you'd like to have in the word search. Now, put the letters of the words horizontally, vertically, or diagonally on a piece of thick paper. See Figure 5.24 for an example.
4. Place that paper with all the letters on top of the nail heads, and push until the paper breaks through. Then wrap rubber bands around the nail heads to do the word search. (You can follow direction for foam-core board word search if it's easier for you than pushing on the nail heads.)

Directions for Foam-Core Board Word Search:

1. Cut a piece of foam-core board into an 8-by-11-inch piece.
2. Place the push-pins into the foam-core board, with seven rows across and down.
3. This will mean there are 49 places for letters.
4. Rub dark-color chalk on top of each push pin and put white cardstock paper on top of the pushpins so the chalk will rub off on it.
5. Accordion-style fold the cardstock paper and using a hole punch, punch a hole where every chalk rub is seen.
6. Unfold the paper and write a letter by each opening.
7. Place the hole-punched paper over the push pins and place rubber bands around the words to identify them on the Geo-Board.
8. Look at Figure 5.24 to see an example of the three-dimensional Geo-Board. Ah, there is a mistake. Can you find it? Clue: The rubber band should be one row up from where it is.

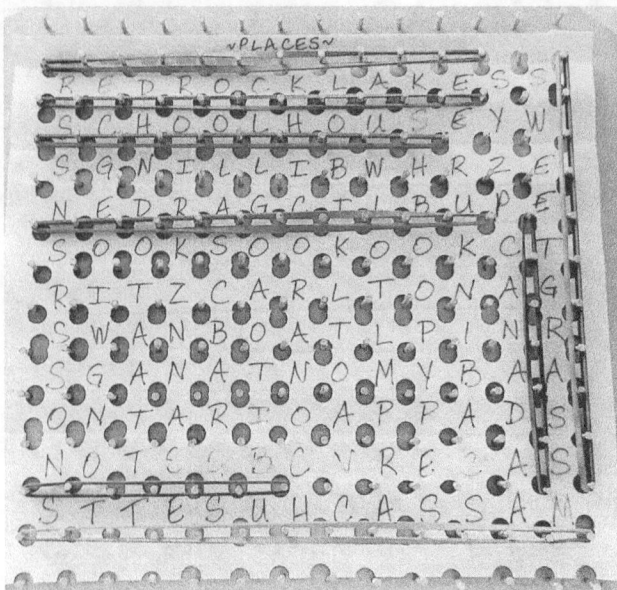

Figure 5.24. Three-Dimensional Super Word Search

"Pic-a-Dot" Do It
Ilyssa Polirer and Catie Mae Rocioppi

This activity is a multiple-choice one that is self-corrective. Directions for how to make this entire interactive instructional resource is in Chapter 9, Figure 9.8. The one seen on this page has math word problems based on the characters in the book *Junie B., First Grader Aloha-ha-ha* by Barbara Park. A card holder is made to hold the cards, which are 5-by-8-inch index cards. About 20 will fit in a holder. The outside of the holder is student-decorated with the theme of the book being addressed.

For the holder, we decided to go with bright colors and stickers representing Hawaii, the setting of the book. Figure 5.25 provides an inside view of one of the cards in its holder. There are also a few other question cards shown. These show how the card with the correct answer has the hole-punched opening going all the way to the bottom of the card.

Figure 5.25. Pic-a-Dot

When using this educational game, just put a pencil point into the hole-punched opening you think is the correct one of the three possible answers provided. Try to pull the card out. If it lifts, then the correct answer has been selected and if not, try again. The cognitive and metacognitive skills from the Reciprocal Thinking Phases are as follows:

Recognizing the topic of the cards are math word problems, *classifying* the subject area, *realizing* this is going to require *analysis*, *risk-taking* when choosing an answer includes *decision-making*, *prioritizing* which of the three choices will answer the question, and *evaluation* through *reflection* and *recalling* how to *problem solve* for *self-actuating*.

Chapter Six

Twenty-Eight Different Ways

The activities in this chapter are a continuation of the previous one, with varied ideas for having interactive classroom instruction. This hands-on type of learning addresses different ways through Interactive Book Reports (IBR) and/or Performance- and/or Project-Based Learning (P/PBL), which calls for student engagement in teaching one's self for the purpose of learning grade-level curriculum. So these activities, as with the first 25 in Chapter 5, are designed to provide not just implementation of one's imagination and creativity but means for retaining what has been presented.

COMMUNICATION: BRAILLE
JOANN LARKIN

The main character, Louis, in the book *Trumpet of the Swans* is born without a voice. Louis is scared to be different from the other swans. He goes away to school with Sam and learns to read and write as well as to communicate with a slate. He writes on the slate with a piece of chalk he wears around his neck. Later, he uses a trumpet to make sounds.

In real life, a person who is born without a voice uses sign language; a person born without sight would learn to read and write Braille. Braille was invented by Louis Braille in 1829, and he was blind. Braille is made up of a rectangular six-dot cell, with up to 63 possible combinations using one or more of the six dots.

Braille is embossed onto thick paper and read with the fingers moving across on top of the dots. Figure 6.1 shows an example of how to write a name with candy dots cut to represent the Braille letters of the name. You'll need some dot candy to try to do this, or you could use poster putty or modeling clay to form the letters. This tactile game is a real-world one. See if you can make a sentence using Braille.

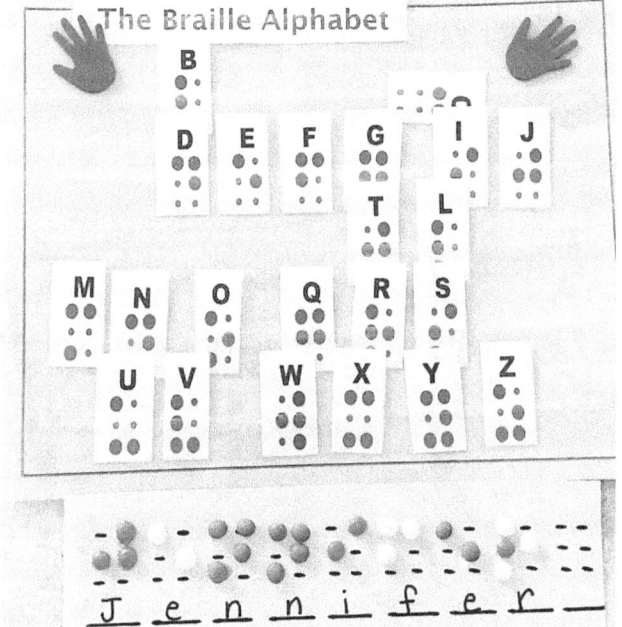

Figure 6.1. Communication: Braille

FACT OR OPINION
BRIANNA HAMMERSCHMITT
AND SAMANTHA SEPE

Realizing the differences between facts and opinions is the main objective of this activity. In the book *Because of Winn Dixie* by Kate DiCamillo, a grocery store–type shopping cart figure was made using a line drawing on paper and then laminating the paper. This shopping cart was used because the main character in the book went shopping at the Winn Dixie grocery store where shopping carts, like in any grocery store, are used to go shopping. One cart was labeled "Facts" and the other "Opinions." The former of these is a true statement and can be supported by printed material or by one being a witness to a situation, so you can testify to its accuracy.

The latter of these two, opinions, are a combination of thoughts and ideas in that a formulated concept results. This is what you think or feel about a situation. Figure 6.2 illustrates the shopping cart shape and has three facts in the Fact Cart and three opinions in the Opinion Cart.

It's your turn to take a book you're reading or some situation you've experienced and make fact and opinion statements. Have at least three of each of these, just like on those in Figure 6.2. On the back put *F* for fact or *O* for opinion, so when someone uses your interactive game, they can self-correct their answers. Trace the shopping cart in Figure 6.2 or come up with two shapes of your own, one for facts and another for opinions. For a real-life situation, you could have "Fact: An orange is a fruit." "Opinion: Many people love the orange's citrus flavor."

MOBILE OF POSITIVE THINKING
SAMANTHA SEPE AND BRIANNA HAMMERSCHMITT

This activity is seeking out the positive things about which you think or have noticed in others' helpful actions. You're asked to reflect on the positives of your life and goals you have. You might even think about how a positive action you took either led to or may lead to a goal you now have. If there doesn't seem to be a connection, then simply put down a goal or two that you have on one of the shapes provided in Figure 6.3. (Of course, you may make your own shape.) This is a whole-class activity where each class member participates individually in the making of a mobile with statements that recognize positive thinking, actions, goals, and noticed positive actions of others.

Materials: Scissors, pen or pencil, shape form, string or yarn or ribbon, clothes hanger, tape, and hole punch. The teacher connects a piece of string to either side of the room so that it runs across the width of the classroom.

Directions:

1. Cut out three shapes on dark-color construction or cardstock paper.
2. Cut out three white pieces of paper to be taped or glued inside the dark color paper.
3. On each one of the white shapes, write one of the following statements.

Statements to Be Addressed:

1. A positive action that someone I know has taken is:
2. A goal I have is:
3. A positive thing I have done is:

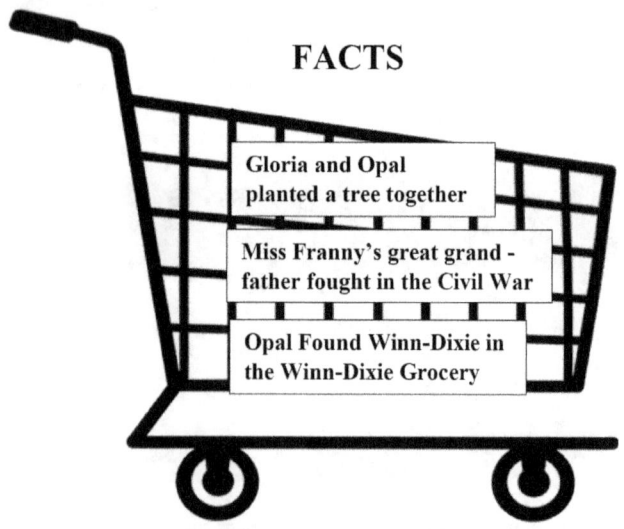

Figure 6.2. Fact or Opinion

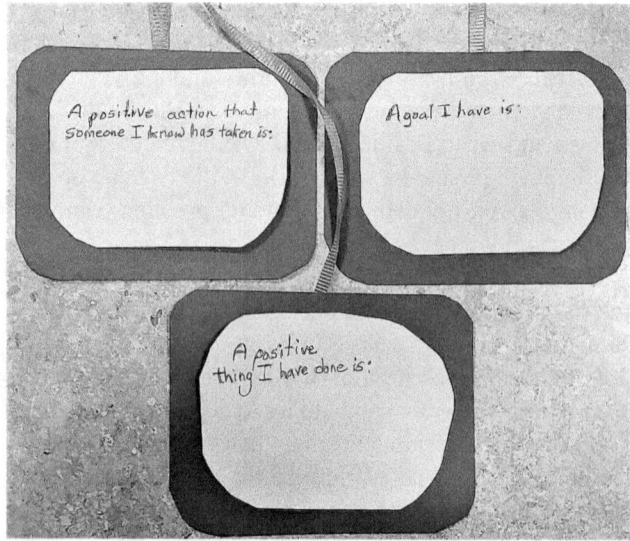

Figure 6.3. Mobile of Positive Thinking

More Directions:

4. Cut 7-inch, 5-inch, and 8-inch pieces of string, yarn, or ribbon.
5. Tape one end on the back of each shape and tie the other end to the bottom of a clothes hanger.
6. Hang the clothes hanger in a place it can be seen by others in the classroom.
7. Read the positives of your classmates and their goals as well. Reread your own positive thinking and goals. Take note of the positives around you in yourself and others. Being surrounded by positive thinking is contagious in that it helps each person realize the positives that frame him or her.

JUMPING THROUGH HOOPS: COMPOUND WORDS
STEVEN LESSIN AND MICHELLE CRONOLLY

This game is designed to have you recognize compound words. You'll need two Hula-Hoops; overlap them on the classroom floor. Make the center section able to hold two 3-by-5-inch index cards side by side. Separate the class into four groups. Each group is to write the first part of five different compound words on an index card and then the second part on another index card. A list of compound words is provided on this page to assist you, but you certainly can have other compound words.

Compound Words: sunshine, breakfast, flowerpot, bullfrog, mailbox, shoestring, skylight, stardust, sandbox, handmade, lifetime, crosswalk, butterflies, weatherman, schoolhouse, classroom, washroom, blackberries, blackboard, bookstore, housekeeper, and grasshopper.

Directions: Each group member, one at a time, jumps into the hoop on the left and places his or her beginning compound word there. Then repeat that for the second part of the word. With the class assisting, each group decides which words go together to form a compound word. Pick up the cards and put both side by side in the overlapping part of the Hula-Hoops.

CHESTER'S WORD SCRAMBLE
STEPHANIE CILLO AND JORDAN NADELL

Oh, no! Chester, the raccoon, stayed up all night making his word board for school the next day. But when he sneezed, all the words were jumbled. Let's help Chester fix his project so he can show everyone his beautiful work. Chester cut out each letter with three different colors to make his words.

Materials: Different color construction paper, pencil, eraser, scissors, Chester's Word Scramble page as seen in Figure 6.5.

Figure 6.5. Chester's Word Scramble

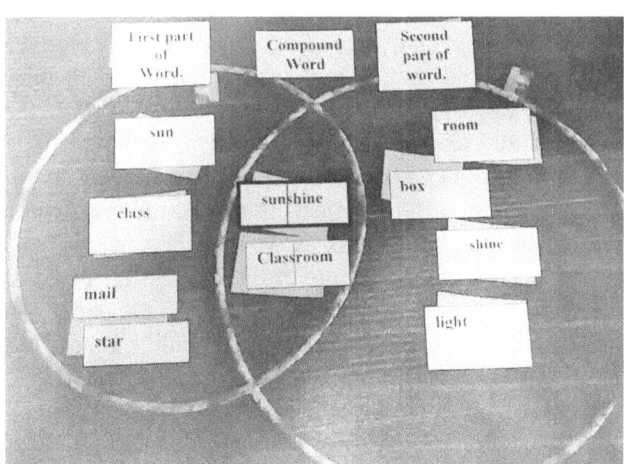

Figure 6.4. Jumping Through Hoops: Compound Words

Directions: Make the word's letters using a different color of construction paper for each letter. Then put the letters on the lines just as shown in Figure 6.5. On another piece of paper, unscramble the words. Think of other words from a book you are reading or words that could be fun to scramble and unscramble. Make a word scramble and see if a classmate can do the unscrambling correctly. Be sure to have an answer sheet for the games you make.

COUNT THE KISSES
STEPHANIE CILLO AND JORDAN NADELL

In the children's book *The Kissing Hand* by Audrey Penn, Chester the Raccoon received his mother's kiss in the center of his hand to remind him that when he went to school he had her love with him. On this electro-board, you are to match, using a continuity tester, the love hearts or numbers on the left side with the correct number or hand hearts on the right side. You'll know if you're correct if the continuity tester lights up when you make your choice.

PERFECT PORTION FOOD GROUPS
SAMANTHA BERNA AND ADAM DEVITO

It is important that we eat food from each food group. A mixture of fruits, vegetables, grains, proteins, and dairy food in your daily diet are good for excellent nutrition. Each food group is labeled for you in Figure 6.7. In the figure, the food groups are named and then a color is attributed to each one.

Figure 6.6. Count the Kisses Electro-Board

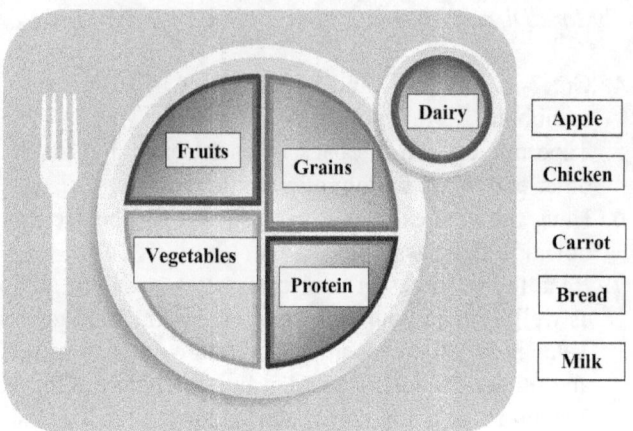

Figure 6.7. Perfect Portions Food Groups

The list of foods on the right side are to be colored the color of the food group in which they belong. Think of foods you eat during the week. To what food groups do they belong? Do you have a healthy diet? For example, in what food group is pizza, cereal, grapes, steak, green beans, tomato, and rice?

WHO IS THE PHILOSOPHER?
MADELINE CRAIG

This is a matching game for all learners and may be modified to a specific ability level depending on the subject area being addressed.

Game Overview: Using matching games in education has been in existence for many years. Young learners play matching games to identify things like shapes, colors, and words. Older learners match words with their definitions using index cards or task cards. In my college courses, I have been using a matching game to help my learners understand course content and in particular to recognize the contributions of key figures by matching who they are to what they said. In one course, Foundations of Education, students play a matching game that asks them to match quotes of famous philosophers to the philosopher and then complete a pamphlet to identify the philosopher, philosophy, and key concepts about the philosophy.

Creating the Game: You will need to create a list of quotes that capture key concepts in your course or in a unit of study in your class, at whatever grade level you teach. You can create a more or less professional type of matching game using a variety of materials: paper and markers, a computer and printer, or an online vendor can create the cards for you.

I chose quotes from educational philosophers for college students in my course. I created PowerPoint slides of each quote. I saved the slides as jpg files so they were in a picture format that Shutterfly would accept as an upload to their website. On Shutterfly, I chose the matching game product and uploaded my jpg files of the quotations. The game looks very professional and the cards are made on hard cardboard and then placed in a decorated box. The cards are then removed from the box and laid out on the floor or tabletop, with the decorative side facing the player.

Alternative Card Construction: You could just as easily use a template in Microsoft Word and print the cards on a quality cardstock to achieve a similar result. Or if you have exceptional penmanship, as many of us teachers do, you could write out the cards yourself.

How to Play the Game: It is important to explain and demonstrate the game carefully to students so they understand the goal of the activity, the learning outcome(s), and how the game will help them learn the course content and, if possible, link it to real-world application. In my case, I explain to the students that it is necessary for them to know the key educational philosophies and the philosophers whose theories still impact education today. I let them know that they will need to know these theories to meet teacher certification requirements and that these ideas should drive what they do as educators in their own classrooms in the future.

Each group of four will play with one matching game and a pamphlet. Players are asked to take turns flipping over two cards until a match is found. Once a match is found, members work together to answer the questions related to that particular quote. I ask them first to try to identify the educational philosophy based on the quote as a type of retrieval practice. Then they are asked to find the philosopher who said the quote using their textbook or mobile device.

Next, players need to identify three key aspects of the philosophy and the philosopher and to write it in their pamphlet. The use of the pamphlet drives this activity to a higher level of thinking. Just matching the quote to the philosopher involves a level of critical thinking since players must consider the words of the quote to determine the features of a particular philosophy and then match it to a philosopher.

For example, a quote that includes ideas related to social justice or equity would require the learner to deduce that the quote can be attributed to the Social Reconstructionism philosophy. Completing the pamphlet requires further thought and explanation of key concepts of the philosophy, thereby requiring groups to perform some research on their mobile devices or in the textbook/articles in the learning management system to discover more about the philosophical school. A simple matching game can therefore be used to differentiate learning for a variety of learners as well as learning outcomes.

Activity Adaptation: What is put for the match may directly relate to different abilities while addressing a specific topic to be studied. For a lower level grade, one might use quotations from a book read in class. Story elements, parts of speech, colors, vocabulary words, opposites, labeled pictures of geographical locations . . . the list could be nearly endless.

Figure 6.8. Who Is the Philosopher?

DOUBLE-DIGIT DELIGHT
CORRINE COOPER AND MEGHAN MOLANO

When it is a hot day in the summer, we think about being cool. Here's a "cool" way to do math problems with Popsicle figures. You'll be adding double-digit numbers and selecting the correct answer card to complete the problem.

Materials: White and other-colored cardstock paper, Velcro tabs, masking tape, 24 Popsicle sticks, and scissors.

Directions:

1. Cut out 12 Popsicle shapes in different colors. I used red, yellow, blue, green, and purple.
2. Print neatly and place a double-digit addition equation on the top part of the cutout.

3. Cover the answer area with a small rectangular piece of white paper and have a Velcro tab on it in the center.
4. Attach two Popsicle sticks to each bottom part of the equation.
5. Cut out 12 rectangular pieces of white paper the size of the ones under the equation on the colored paper and write the answer to each equation on one of these pieces of white paper.
6. Check your answers with a partner or the teacher. Put the equation it addresses on the back in small print. This is so when others are working the equations, the player can self-correct by turning over the answer to see if he or she put it with the correct equation.
7. Put a Velcro tab on the back side of the paper and place the answer under the equation (Velcro to Velcro) where it answers the Popsicle stick addition problem.
8. Using masking tape on the back of the Popsicle stick equation, tape these to the classroom board. Use Figure 6.9 to see how this looks when completed.

DINOSAUR SUBTRACTION GAME
MEGHAN MOLANO AND CORRINE COOPER

Here's a fun game using subtraction. To make it, you'll need to make a game board as shown in Figure 6.10; you can enlarge it on a photocopier. Get a pair of dice as you follow the directions on how to play this game.

Directions: Each player puts a marker on start. These can be any small object such as those pictured in Figure 6.10. If you choose to make markers, then cut out the shape and mount it on thick paper. Or your marker could be an eraser, paper clip, sticky tack shaped like a square, and so on.

Two players take turns rolling one die. Move forward that many spaces. Answer the subtraction problem. Cover that answer on the volcano in the center of the game board. Do this with your marker. If the number is covered, then that player (one or two) will not cover any number on that round. If you land on a dinosaur, any number of your choice can be covered in the center of the board. The winner is the player who covers the last number on the volcano.

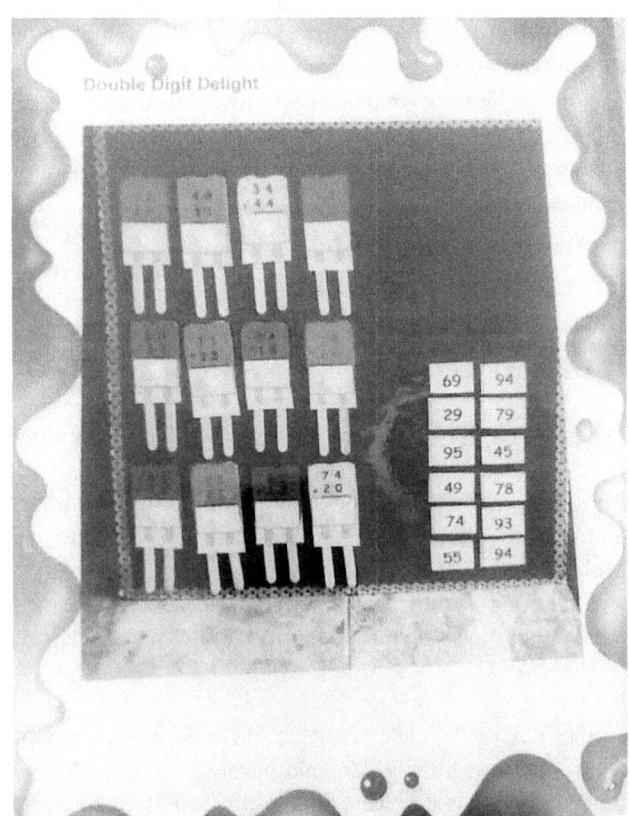

Figure 6.9. Double-Digit Delight

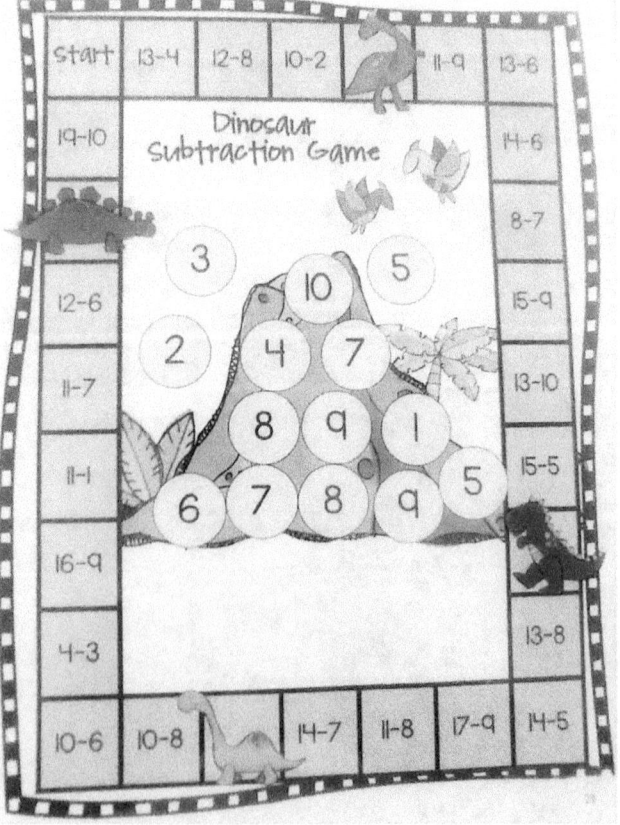

Figure 6.10. Dinosaur Subtraction Game

BUTTERFLY FLIP-CHUTE
MICHELLE LEBLANC AND KATIE BERNSTEIN

This activity is designed to help you review vocabulary words that are related to butterflies as well as their life cycle. The directions for making a flip-chute and flip-chute cards are found in Chapter 9, Figure 9.6. Follow those directions and view Figure 9.7 for an already constructed and designed flip-chute.

Directions After Making Flip-Chute and Flip-Chute Cards:

1. Take one of the cards and read the definition. Refer to the vocabulary list at the end of this activity to figure out what word best fits that definition.
2. Into the top chute, insert the card, with the notch on the upper right side. Make sure the definition is facing up so that you can read it. Let go of the card. When the card comes out the bottom chute, your answer will be showing.
3. This is a self-corrective activity. So make a pile of the cards you missed getting correct and review them by repeating steps 1 and 2. Be sure to go through all of the vocabulary words as many times as you need. Everyone learns at a different pace! This is not a race!

Vocabulary List:

Larva: another word for caterpillar
Abdomen: hind portion of the body of an insect
Butterfly: slender-bodied flying insects with large, bright, symmetrically colored wings
Life Cycle: series of changes in the life of an organism
Egg: the first stage of a butterfly's life
Antennas: movable feelers on the heads of insects
Cocoon: a silky case spun by an insect in the larva stage
Chrysalis: the third stage of a butterfly's life cycle
Pupa: the middle stage of an insect's development
Species: a class of living things of the same kind that have the same name
Environment: the surroundings in which a person, plant, or animal lives
Metamorphosis: a significant change that an animal or insect goes through, such as a caterpillar becoming a butterfly
Caterpillar: long, worm-like stage of the butterfly's life

Figure 6.11. Butterfly Flip-Chute

WHEEL OF ADJECTIVES
KATIE BERNSTEIN AND MICHELLE LEBLANC

This educational game is provided to familiarize you with adjectives. These are words that describe nouns. The unit on butterflies gave us many adjectives when describing this insect during its life cycle.

Materials: Poster board, scissors, 12 clothes pins, computer, and/or markers.

Directions:

1. Make a wheel/circle from poster board that is 9 inches in diameter.
2. Using your computer, make 12 text boxes that are 1 inch wide by 1½ inches long.
3. Inside the text boxes, write one of the 12 descriptive sentences displayed in step 7 of this list of directions.

4. Cut out the 12 text boxes and paste them onto the circle near the outer edge.
5. Write the same descriptive word that appears in the sentence on each of 12 clothes pins and clip the clothes pin onto the wheel where that adjective appears in a sentence.
6. If you have other sentences and adjectives you'd like to use, feel free to do that.
7. The *tired* butterfly took a nap on a leaf. The butterfly flew over the *pretty* lake. The *large* caterpillar ate all of the delicious food. A *little* girl found a small butterfly egg on a leaf. The chrysalis swayed in the *strong* gusts of wind. It was a *sunny* day when the caterpillar turned into a butterfly. The butterfly landed on the bright *green* plant. The caterpillar felt *fuzzy*. The butterfly's wings are *purple*. The *tiny* caterpillar became a butterfly. The *hungry* caterpillar ate two flowers. That is a *colorful* butterfly.

name of the state. If the light lights up, you selected the correct answer. If you want to make an electro-board, see Chapter 9, Figure 9.10 for directions. A suggestion is to "capitalize" on this game and make one of your own with all 50 states!

New York State Learning Standard 3.7: Whereas physical features and natural features are created by the environment, political features are human constructions such as national boundaries, cities, and states.

Figure 6.13. Know Some States—Electro-Board

MAP SECTION DIRECTIONS
BRITTANY GERVASE AND MADISON GERAGHTY

Our friend Stuart was going from New York City's Madison Square Garden to Lincoln Center. He needed a map, so we got one for him, as you can see at the end of Activity 14. The path he took has been outlined, and it's your job to use the compass rose and, talking with a classmate, say what directions he traveled from the starting point to the ending one. Now here's a challenge. Write some directions of your own by beginning at Madison Square Garden and ending at a place of your choice. Then, write down the directions for a partner and see if he or she can draw a line and state the directions traveled to get to your ending point.

Example: (1) Starting at Madison Square Garden, you are to go to (2) Times Sq. (Square) and then to (3) the Empire State Building (Bld.). Travel from that location over to (4) Third where it touches the left tip of the letter *W* on the compass rose. Now proceed in a straight line to

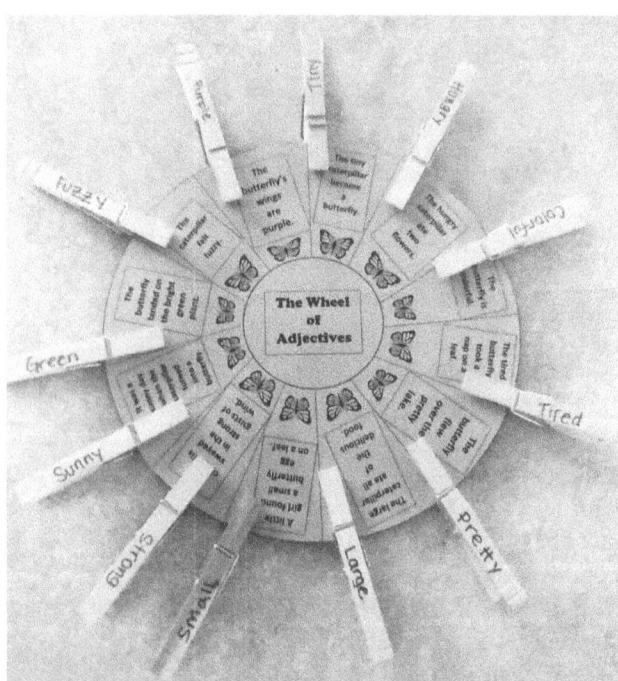

Figure 6.12. Wheel of Adjectives

KNOW SOME STATES—ELECTRO-BOARD
JESSICA TRINIDAD AND MARGARET LIGUORI

In the book we read in class today, the main character visited places in the south of the United States and traveled a bit west as well. This electro-board has you using a continuity tester by holding it in one hand and then putting the tip of the tester on an answering brass fastener and placing the index finger of your other hand on the

(5) 53rd and go to (6) the Museum of Modern Art. How many directions did you travel, and what were they? The answers are at the end of Rhyme Weave-Around. Have fun!

Sight Word Vocabulary: can, me, down, crack, little, my, you, that, knows, squish, do, let, talk, you're, please, to, our, hurt, shoe, crumb, change, up, decide, is, say, your, crazy, speck, around, too, flat, and, anyone. (These were our words, make your own list.)

Answer Key: Roll a Sight Word

2 Letters	3 Letters	4 Letters	5 Letters	6 Letters
me	can	down	crack	little
my	you	that	knows	squish
do	let	talk	you're	please
to	and	shoe	crumb	change
up	too	flat	close	anyone
of	say	hurt	crazy	decide
is	our	your	speck	around

Figure 6.15. Roll a Sight Word

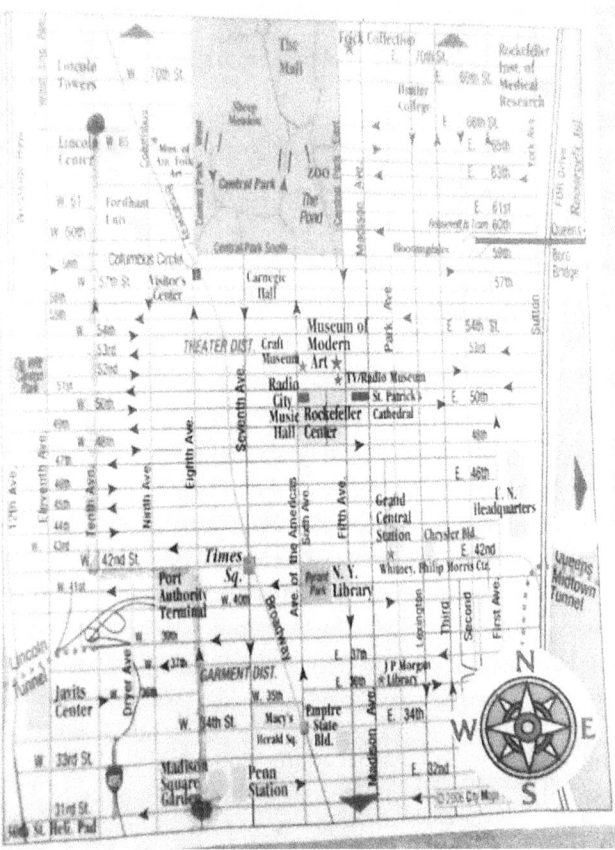

Figure 6.14. Map Section Directions

ROLL A SIGHT WORD
ALEXIS CORREA AND EMMA KAISER

Sight words help readers read more fluently while increasing vocabulary and understanding of new or commonly used words at varied grade levels. This tactile activity requires a die, Sight Word List, and Word Letter Number Chart (see Figures 6.15).

Roll the die and see what number it lands on. Find a sight word from the list that has the same number of letters as dots on the die. Write the word in dry-erase marker on the laminated Sight Word List, in the two-, three-, four-, five-, or six-letter column. Of course, this depends on the number of letters in the word and the die number you rolled. Cross off the words that you use on your Sight Word List before you make another roll. If you want to have words that have more than six letters, use two die. That could be challenging but also applicable for upper grades or students with different abilities who are considered gifted and/or talented.

RHYME WEAVE-AROUND
BILLY BUSHNELL AND JOSEPH ESPOSITO

This weave-around is designed to have you recognizing words that have the same ending sounds and last letters. We have six shown in Figure 6.16, but you could make one with more. This mostly tactile activity engages you

Figure 6.16. Rhyming Word Matching Wraparound

in putting yarn or string through the opening, which is just below the word on the left side, and matching it by weaving the yarn through to the opening below the rhyming word, which is just beneath the word on the right side. Weave away!

(*Answers to Map Section Directions example*: Started at Madison Square Garden and traveled northeast, then southeast, east, north, and west.)

IS IT MAGNETIC OR NOT?
CAITLIN BAER AND RYAN PEARSALL

This activity is a matching game where we chose to make an electro-board. However, here you're asked to either make one of these or make a wraparound, as seen in Chapter 9, Figure 9.9. Then again, you might want to create your own pic-a-dot with multiple-choice answers or make a weave-around, which is nearly the same as a wraparound, only holes are punched near but not at the border, so the yarn may be woven through these openings to connect the question on the left with the correct answer on the right. Or you might want to make a set of task cards where matching is done by shape.

Our electro-board (see Figure 6.17) has six things that may be magnetic, which relates to or exhibits magnetism/ capable of being magnetized and results in the magnet sticking to an object. But *nonmagnetic* refers to there being no magnetic pull. For example, a magnet held to metal would stick but would not stick to one's skin, as skin is nonmagnetic. So using the guide provided, you're invited to make your own interactive instructional resource on magnets, and please don't limit yourself to 6 items but try to have 10 or more.

POINT OF VIEW: ELEMENTS OF CHARACTERIZATION
HELEN GAVIN

This sample activity lesson incorporates previous learning and targets New York State Learning Standards for English language arts in the following areas: Reading Standards, Writing, Speaking, and Learning. Careful preparation is crucial for success in the classroom, and using active reading and writing strategies will embrace and develop areas of strength and identify and address students' individual areas of need.

This English 7 inclusion class of 21 students is composed of both regular education students and classified students with individual education programs (IEPs). The classified students' IEPs were reviewed and information was used to plan for classroom modifications and testing accommodations. All of the students, I think, benefit from the scaffolding of lessons and from attention to their increasing metacognitive skills to gain an understanding of their personal learning preferences.

Prior to this lesson, it's advised that the novel *Pay It Forward* by Catherine Ryan Hyde be read. The novel focuses on a character who is assigned a social studies project that has the potential for effecting change on a world level. The specific learning target is focused on point of view and how identifying elements of characterization and evaluating them can assist the reader in comprehension of the author's message. This is from the viewpoint of the main character or may be from the point of view of others in the story.

Directions: First Activity Viewpoint

1. Students watch a short film clip of *The True Story of Three Little Pigs* by A. Wolf, a version of the classic fairy tale told from the point of view of the wolf (https://www.youtube.com/watch?v=vB07RfntTvw).
2. An entrance ticket will be completed to display student knowledge of point of view/perspective and to prepare students for thinking-skills whole-class activities on knowledge of the literary technique, a point of view.

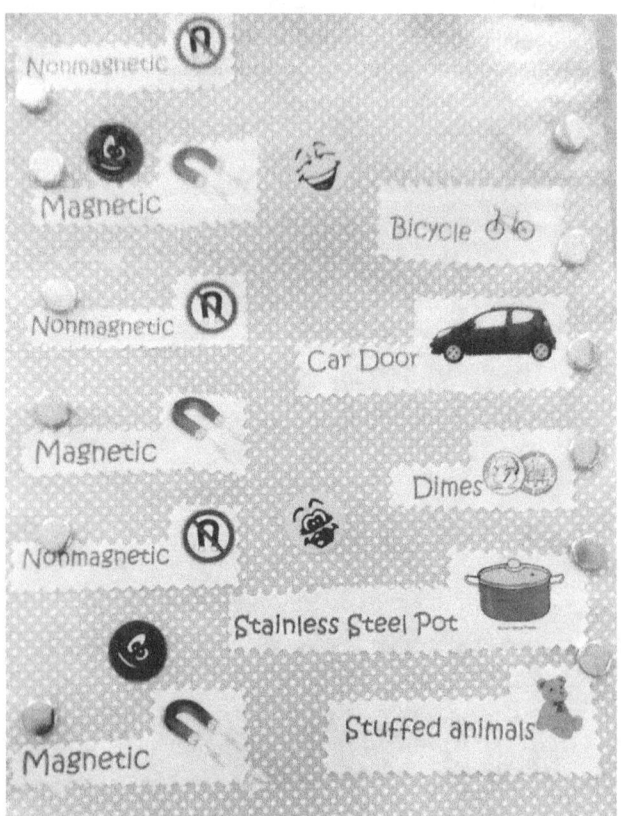

Figure 6.17. Magnetic-Nonmagnetic Electro-Board

Name:

This video clip shows a different point of view from the traditional fairytale "The Three Little Pigs." Write one sentence explaining how the change in the point of view affects the story.

The change point of view affects the story because each point of view has a different type of telling the story. The wolf had to get sugar. Also asking for sugar.

Figure 6.18. Point of View

3. Students independently write at least one sentence explaining how a change in point of view affects the story.

Directions: Second Activity Viewpoint: After completing the assignment on viewpoint from the wolf's perspective in the classic story of *The Three Little Pigs*, the students are assigned to three different abilities groups. Each group has a tier assignment, moving from basic awareness of realizing to critical thinking of decision-making to metacognitive processes of reflecting and self-actuating.

The groups range in ability level from independent to those who need a good deal of assistance. The students are given the assignment of completing an activity where they examine a photograph of many people on a crowded street. Such a photograph can be obtained from the internet. What follows are the tiers of this assignment:

- Students recognize the setting and characters in the picture.
- Then, they are to discuss and analyze the photograph to determine what is happening in it.
- Next, these students will randomly choose a card on the table, designating a person in the picture.
- Each student is to write a one to two paragraph narrative story. The story is about the photograph. The viewpoint is from the perspective of the character on the card they have and who is in the picture with the others.
- Stories are shared with the class.

GEOMETRIC SHAPES: A MATH WORD PROBLEM FLOOR GAME
MARJORIE SCHIERING

Using a shower curtain liner and a black permanent marker, draw the shapes seen in Figure 6.19. Be sure to do this in the same order as shown. To play this game, you need to remove your shoes and answer the equations presented below by stepping on the shape that represents the numbers that involve addition, multiplication, subtraction, or division. What you're doing is walking the parts of the word problem to come to the answer. As you do each part, say what's being done, as shown below in the parentheses at the end of steps 1 through 5.

What if the answer is a larger number than any number on the shapes on the floor game? Let's say the answer is 24 and there are only shapes with 1–10 on them. An example of what to do would be to have the player step two times on the number 10 and one time on the number 4. Or you could step on the numbers 2 and 4, if they are not too far apart.

The Reciprocal Thinking Skills for this activity are *recognizing* the rules of the game and the geometrical shapes while *classifying* them. *Organization* of the steps to be taken, whether addition or one of the other three operations, is done when walking the parts of the equation. *Generalizing* is evidenced with the types of questions being in the math discipline and *problem-solving* and *decision-making* are necessary to get the correct answer to the equation. *Reflecting* on answers and self-actuating is realized when the answer is stated.

Ten Sample Word Problem Questions:

1. What is the sum of the square and the oval (1 + 6)?
2. How much is the cylinder times the star minus the triangle (3 × 7 –10)?
3. What is the circle multiplied by the crescent divided by the cylinder (5 × 6 ÷ 3)?
4. How much is a cube plus the rectangle times the hexagon (4 + 2 × 8)?
5. When you add the diamond to the star and take away the oval, what do you have as a shape and number answer (11 + 7 – 6)?
6. What is the sum of each of the shapes on the floor game (1 + 2 + 3 + 4 + 5 + 6 + 7 + 8 + 9 + 10 + 11)?
7. If you subtract the triangle from the diamond and add the cylinder and the crescent, what shapes do you have and what's the number in that shape (11 – 10 + 3 + 9)?
8. Tom had five circles and he added a triangle and then multiplied this by the square. What number did he have as the answer to this equation (25 + 10 × 1)?
9. If the girl had six stars and then five stars were taken away and these were multiplied by the rectangle and divided by the rectangle, what shape would you have and what number is in that shape (6 × 7 – 5 × 7 × 2 ÷ 2)?
10. There are 10 triangles and 2 cylinders, which are divided by a square. What shapes do you have and what's the number in that shape (10 × 10 + 6 ÷ 1)?

I CAN RECYCLE
AMANDA MINOGUE AND MARYKATE MURNANE

Recycling paper, cans, and plastic is really important for us to do! Why? It's because we want to keep our Earth clean. Every year our country has a day called Earth Day. We dedicate our time to how our Earth can be kept safe. This activity involves constructing three lift-up paper bins where we classify items that would go into each one.

Materials: Two sheets of laminated cardstock paper; red, yellow, and blue markers; the recycle sign; three circle shapes; tape; at least four pictures of paper, metal/tin containers, and plastic items, Velcro tabs.

Directions: Make a poster like the one in Figure 6.20 and put the tape at the top of each drawn bin so you can lift it. Draw or get pictures of items that are in each of

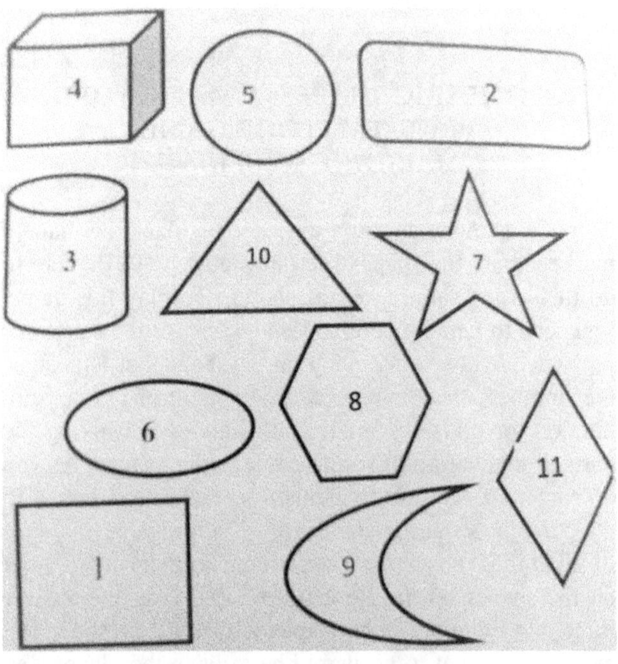

Figure 6.19. Geometric Shape Word Problems

Figure 6.20. I Can Recycle

the aforementioned categories, the ones labeled on the illustration of the bins on the poster. Put Velcro tabs on each item and at least four inside the bin. However, put in more tabs and Velcro more items if you can. Now, on the back of each picture, color code it with a line the color of each bin so those playing this game can check whether they put the recyclable item in the correct bin. Be part of the antipollution idea and be sure to *recycle*!

HOMES—YESTERDAY AND TODAY
CLARE KING

This activity calls for you to do some drawing and describing. The setting of the book I was reading was at a house in the woods. And the time of the story was during pioneer days. The houses back then were very different from today, as there weren't houses next to each other and there were no apartment buildings either. For this activity, you'll need to do some research about how houses appeared back in the 1800s.

So have a look using the internet and maybe find a website or two that tells you about the time of pioneers and those who traveled westward to settle in a new area. When you've done that, use the template in Figure 6.21 and write a few descriptive statements about a house in pioneer times. Then, using an exterior drawing of the place you live or again using the template provided, write about where you live. Compare the two and add a picture of your present home on the inside. You're invited to share your descriptive writing and pictures with friends and/or family.

BIOLOGY: FOOD WEBS: SPECIAL EDUCATION GRADES 7–12
RYAN LANE

One lesson in which I successfully incorporated activity-based strategies to facilitate student learning was a lesson in a self-contained high school science class on the food web. Primarily, this used modeling to demonstrate the interconnectedness of members in an ecosystem. Understanding the interactions of organisms within an environment, particularly the dynamics of a food web and energy transfer within an ecosystem, are critical to being successful in most life science classes. This theme spans across grade levels and is a key component in the Next Generation Science Standards.

To that end, this lesson guides students through the process of creating a class-wide model of a food web using "role cards" and string to demonstrate the interdependence of organisms in an ecosystem.

The lesson begins with students viewing a video of various predators hunting their prey. This serves as an engaging activity for the students that gets them interested and invested in the lesson. It also activates their prior knowledge and provides the teacher with an assessment on how much students know about the topic. The discussion is used to ensure students have a basic understanding of some key vocabulary terms that they will need in order to successfully construct the model (*predator*, *prey*, *producer*, and *consumer*). Figure 6.22 has the model and questions are below.

Figure 6.21.   Homes—Yesterday and Today

Figure 6.22.   A Food Web

Food Web Questions

Name of my organism by type (**producer** or **consumer**) _____
The **PREDATOR** is _____
I am a **predator** of _____
The **PREY** is _____
I am the **prey** of _____

Questions to Consider about the Food Web:

1. Since the producers don't have any prey, from where do you think they get their energy?
2. Explain what would happen to a fruit fly population if the thrush went extinct.

After the discussion, the teacher distributes a food web worksheet that students use throughout the remainder of the lesson. The students use their role cards, yarn, and scissors to create a model of a food web. Each student will also receive one role card.

The front side of the role card has an image and the name of an organism, while the reverse lists the predators and prey of that specific organism (when applicable). Students begin filling out their worksheets as they identify the role of their organism (producer or consumer) as well as rewrite the list of predators and prey. Students are instructed to find the students with role cards representing their organism's prey or predators and to each hold one end of a piece of yarn. Students are given the general instruction that their organism must be connected to each of its predators and prey, but how to construct the model is left to the discretion of the students.

Students should be given sufficient time to explore the different role cards available and collaborate with their peers to determine the best procedure to establish all of the correct connections. Allowing the students to do this on their own helps develop the habits of mind and skills necessary for a 21st-century learner, such as problem-solving, critical thinking, collaboration, and communication.

See links to the student worksheet as well as the role cards described above.

https://drive.google.com/open?id=1UhaFTug4_EqYz0R5Q2hZnURySKEiSqq7AO3A40iruK8
https://drive.google.com/open?id=1UWOgYx2pK7raBAHsTabZYJ1KTH01nyCIhYDJYFoSR5Y

Once the model is complete and all string connections are made, the class is led in a discussion about the connectedness of the organisms in the food web. Next, the class has a simulation of environmental stressors that are believed to be put on the organisms in an ecosystem when populations decline or become extinct because of human impact and other factors. This can be achieved by selecting one student to sit on the floor with their strings while the other members of the food web remain standing.

Doing this causes the connections to become distorted as the overlapping strings are pulled downward. From this simulation, students are able to easily conclude that when the population of one organism in an ecological community decreases, the entire food web is also affected.

The demonstration allows the students to build knowledge through experience and exploration, as they draw conclusions on their own before the content is reinforced by the teacher. Differentiation and adaptations are evident throughout the entire lesson. All students are provided with guided notes to use during the direct instruction of the content. The notes have fill-in-the-blank bullets and pictures that coincide with the PowerPoint to help students remain on task and focused during the presentation. In terms of the assessment at the end of the lesson, ability levels for differentiation are addressed. These include:

1. Struggling learners may be provided with sentence starters to assist them when completing the five questions on the worksheet (i.e., "The most important member of this food web is the _____ because . . .").
2. The middle group answers the first three questions (multiple choice) and also are required to provide written responses for numbers 4 and 5, which appear on the worksheet on the "hyperlink" that leads to the website.
3. The higher level students research a local ecosystem where the food web has been disrupted or sketch a diagram of the food web with a written explanation in their science journals.

By having an interactive lesson and giving attention, this strategy enhances students' comprehension of a complex topic by making it relatable, tangible, and accessible to them.

ROTATION OF A GEOMETRIC SHAPE
NETTA RIBA

This activity provides experience with geometric concepts. It can be used independently or to supplement classroom instruction regarding the rotation of geometric shapes. See Figure 6.23 for a visual of this rotation.

Materials:

1. Two pieces of tracing paper
2. A sheet of medium-weight plastic (e.g., an overhead projector sheet, one side of a page-protector, the plastic sheet from a new shirt or, about 10 inches of medium-weight plastic sheeting from a hardware store) (*Note:* Never draw in the middle of the plastic sheet as it wastes space and prevents other drawings. Draw as close to one side as possible.)
3. One thin-line permanent marker. (If the marker is not permanent, it will smear on the plastic. If needed, permanent marker can be erased with a tissue dampened with rubbing alcohol. Alcohol will also remove permanent marker from clothing.)
4. Scissors
5. A small bottle of rubbing alcohol
6. A ruler

Definitions:

1. *Square:* A four-sided figure all of whose angles are right angles and all of whose sides are the same length
2. *Scalene Triangle:* A triangle all of whose sides are of different lengths

Directions:

1. Using the upper left-hand corner, draw a small square (about 1 inch on a side) on the plastic with the permanent marker and a ruler and label it ABCD as shown in #1 in Figure 6.23.
2. Cut out the square, leaving enough space around it to include the letters.
3. Place a dot somewhere inside the square, not in the center.
4. Trace the square, letters, and dot in the upper left-hand corner of the tracing paper. Do not press too hard to avoid ripping the tracing paper.
5. Rotate the square so that the letters are now positioned as in illustration #2.
6. Trace the square, letters, and dot next to the first drawing.
7. Continue to rotate and trace the square until the dot returns to its original position.

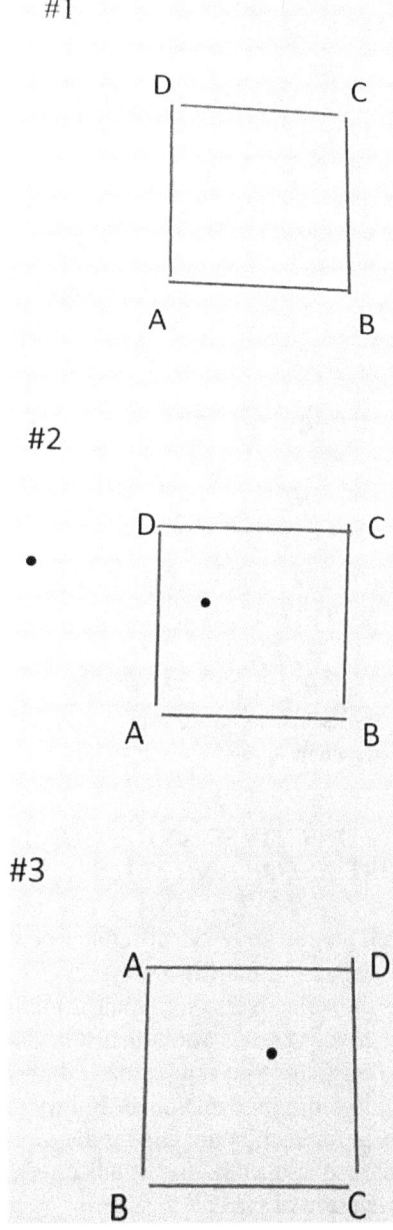

Figure 6.23. Rotation of a Geometric Shape

FRACTION ACTION
KELSEY CRAPO AND MARISSA SCIACCA

For this activity, we are going to put our fraction knowledge to the test! Using a picture of a colored-in wheel, match it up to the fraction that expresses how much of the wheel is shaded. You will know you are correct when you put the cards together and it is a match. Your instructions are to have the following fractions and make a shape for each one. Fill in/color in the portion that represents each of the fractions.

20 Fractions: 1/2, 1/3, 1/4, 1/5, 1/6, 1/7, 1/8, 1/9, 1/10, 2/4, 2/3, 3/4, 3/8, 6/10, 12/15, 10/11, 5/6, 2/5, 9/10, 4/5.

See if you can find equivalent fractions that are in this list of 20 fractions.

Figure 6.24. Fraction Action

ADJECTIVES AND NOUNS
BROOKE ASTOR AND MADISON DODD

Just how well do you know the difference between nouns and adjectives? Using the list of adjectives below, draw a line from the adjective to the noun it might describe. Remember adjectives are words that tell you about the noun. You'll find that you can correctly draw a line from an adjective to more than one noun. But try to limit it to two adjectives for each noun. Give it a try and copy this list of words and add to the list of adjectives and nouns on a separate piece of paper.

Adjectives	Nouns
blue	elephant
large	school
friendly	computer
beautiful	television
artful	box
round	crayon
impressive	toy
green	cat
first	door
last	room
stinky	lion

CHARACTER TRAIT: ROLE-PLAY AWAY...
MARJORIE SCHIERING

Directions: This activity involves kinesthetic/whole-body movement for acting out the provided situations. The idea is to have a few classmates and yourself get together and *pretend* you're in one of the situations stated in scenarios 1–5. These need to have an ending that represents being a person of good character. These are represented by the words and actions of being one or some of the following in what you say or do: kind, fair, trustworthy, responsible, respectful, and a good citizen. Each scene requires a decision, so you will need to use your imagination as to what's the right thing to do. There is no script, unless you really want to make one.

The idea is to present your role-play to the class and see if they can guess which character trait(s) your group represented in your acting. (Remember that being fair is not about everyone getting the same thing or what one wants but about getting what one needs. Now use the dictionary and look up the meaning for the other five character traits.)

Scenarios:

1. The neighbor's dog got loose and is running across your yard, you go outside to catch her and succeed. But your neighbor is not home, so you can't return the dog. How old are the characters in this scene, and what is done?
2. There was a time when you saw your friend being bullied by two classmates. Being a person of good character, what did you say or do?
3. Gym class is pretty hectic and you're doing jumping jacks when you notice the person next to you is getting exhausted and seems to be about to faint. What do you do?
4. Your friend has just told you a secret about how she's going to "get back at" the kids that made her miss the math test by stopping her from going to class. She's really upset and plans to "make them pay" by hurting them. What do you say and do?
5. There are nine people needed to play the game and you, as captain, have only eight people present. There are five people wanting and waiting to be on the team. How to you select the two people for the team? What's your criteria and your motivation?
6. The ice-cream truck has come to a stop by your house. You have just enough money to get two ice creams, but both your sister and brother are there and want one. What do you say and do?
7. The algebra test in math class has just been distributed and you are quite the math genius. Your friend

leans over and asks to see your paper. What do you say and do?
8. There is an army of ants that has invaded the kitchen counter and you are terrified of them. But they are about to take over the entire counter and no one is home. What do you say or do?
9. One of your parents has grounded you for the week because you were late getting home. But you think this is unfair because you wouldn't have been late if your friend had picked you up on time. You think the grounding punishment is unfair. You want to plead your case to the other parent but hesitate and decide to speak to both parents. What do you say?
10. This one is up to you. With two classmates, select a scenario that has an ending of being a very caring, good citizen.

WHERE DO I LIVE?
JOSEPH ESPOSITO AND WILLIAM BUSHNELL

Do you know that most living things have a habitat and so do objects? A habitat is the place where things live, and their specific place is called a *niche*. This is your chance to use your drawing skills or the internet for making or getting pictures. The idea of this activity is to recognize the stated animal, insect, plant, or object. Next get 10 single pieces of paper and write the name of your living thing or object on the paper and do a drawing of it. Where you put those on the paper is up to you.

Next, make an illustration of where the animal, insect, plant, or object's habitat is or its niche in that specific place. You may choose to use the computer to find pictures of where the animal or insect or plant lives. When you're done, share your activity with a classmate or a few of them or the whole class. When you've finished creating each illustrated page, bind it together and title your booklet's cover "Who I Am and Where I Live."

Example: A human being's habitat may be on a street in a community. Its niche would be a house on that street.

EARTH DAY HISTORY
MARYKATE MURNANE AND AMANDA MINOGUE

For this activity, you'll need to have information about Earth Day. Where can you find it? Two suggestions are from a class textbook or the internet. See how many fill-ins you can do, and then make a poster about keeping our Earth clean through recycling, reducing, and reusing! Share your posters by placing them on a display board in your classroom or at home. Use the Word/Statement Bank to help you do the fill-ins correctly.

Earth Day was first celebrated in _____ and is celebrated on _____. On this day, we remember to care for our _____ and it is _____. Over _____ participate in this celebration. The Earth is a very special place and it is the only known _____ where life can be found. This is because it has _____ and _____. Without these, living things could not exist. Earth Day is the _____ in the world. On this day, many people come to celebrate and show appreciation for the _____. They do this by being part of a service project, such as _____, _____, _____, and __ _____.

Word and Statement Bank: April 22, planet, 1970, Earth, recycling, oxygen, moderate temperatures, water, natural resources, picking up trash, planting trees and flowers, 100 countries, cleaning up abandoned areas.

Chapter Seven

Different Ways with 13 Examples
Technology

The first set of activities in this chapter are specifically designed for interaction with the computer. These contributions are from teacher candidates in various classes provided by Rickey Moroney over several years of teaching technology at Molloy College. The remainder of the activities are at various grade levels and have been created by graduate students in the Division of Education at Molloy.

POWER OF THE INTERNET: LONG ISLAND DURING THE AMERICAN REVOLUTION: E-TEXTBOOK CHAPTER
RICKEY MORONEY
http://revolutionarylongisland.weebly.com/

The next few activities, after this one, are those presented by teachers using web quests they personally designed. The power of the internet as a research tool is all encompassing; well-constructed assignments have the power to motivate and engage today's learners in dynamic ways that conventional resources of old never could.

From web quests to QR code scavenger hunts to virtual field trips, a variety of tools, strategies, methods, and assessments are available for the teacher and learner to use in unique ways. One can only speculate what the future holds with the emergence of VR (virtual reality), AR (augmented reality), and MR (mixed reality); these tools promise experiences that will engage the learner intellectually, *interactively/physically*, emotionally, and socially in almost unimaginable ways.

Inexpensive tools such as the Merge Cube, apps like Mr. Body, and a smartphone with a VR headset can take students on a journey through an age-appropriate interactive learning experience of the systems of the human body. AI (artificial intelligence) also offers us the convenience of learning and interacting with technology in more active rather than conventional passive modalities.

How often do we ask Siri or Alexa questions or request information? These opportunities for learning will offer us unconventional teaching for students who have different abilities. When? Anytime, anywhere, as students become problem-solvers, creators, and producers rather than just consumers of information.

What Is a Web Quest?

A web quest is an internet-based research project. It emphasizes higher order thinking (such as analysis, synthesis, or evaluation) rather than just the acquisition of information. How the information is used is stressed, instead of conventional research-gathering tasks. Most web quests are completed cooperatively by small groups and the tasks are divided into roles.

Web quests have a standard format and include an introduction, task (what the students will produce), process (steps the students should take to complete the task), resources (online resources), evaluation (specific criteria for judgment, such as a rubric), and conclusion.

The web quest was conceived and developed by Bernie Dodge in 1995 and is still a vibrant and viable activity that can be used in today's classrooms; some newer additions might include the use of scanned QR codes to lead students to find the information resources that they need to accomplish their tasks.

This e-textbook chapter, created as part of the fourth-grade social studies curriculum, focuses on local events and significant figures of the period. Students use this in lieu of a traditional textbook to interact with the material provided; they learn through historical pictures, videos, audio highlighting music of the period, word clouds, activities, and collaborative projects. Rubrics are provided for the projects and activities. Parents are also included in the process by helping and supporting their children while they complete the chapter's varied and diverse content activities and projects, such as Heroes and Spies, which has students form spy rings like the Culper Spy Ring to go on a mission and write a report for General George Washington.

Standards Addressed

New York State Learning Standards Social Studies Grades K–8

Standard 1: History of the United States and New York Students will use a variety of intellectual skills to demonstrate their understanding of major ideas, eras, themes, developments, and turning points in the history of the United States and New York.

Standard 3: Geography Students will use a variety of intellectual skills to demonstrate their understanding of the geography of the interdependent world in which we live—local, national, and global—including the distribution of people, places, and environments over the Earth's surface.

Standard 5: Civics, Citizenship, and Government Students will use a variety of intellectual skills to demonstrate their understanding of the necessity for establishing governments; the governmental system of the United States and other nations; the United States Constitution; the basic civic values of American constitutional democracy; and the roles, rights, and responsibilities of citizenship, including avenues of participation.

Common Core State Standards Initiative: English Language Arts Standards, Reading: Informational Text, Grade 4, Key Ideas and Details

RI.4.1. Refer to details and examples in a text when explaining what the text says explicitly and when drawing inferences from the text.

RI.4.2. Determine the main idea of a text and explain how it is supported by key details; summarize the text.

RI.4.3. Explain events, procedures, ideas, or concepts in a historical, scientific, or technical text, including what happened and why, based on specific information in the text.

ISTE NETS for Students

3. Research and Information Fluency Students apply digital tools to gather, evaluate, and use information. Students: b. locate, organize, analyze, evaluate, synthesize, and ethically use information from a variety of sources and media.

The "Long Island During the American Revolution" e-textbook chapter can be found at http://revolutionarylongisland.weebly.com/.

THE CRADLE OF WESTERN CIVILIZATION: ANCIENT GREECE: WEB QUEST
CHRISTINA CEDRONE
http://ancientgreecequest.weebly.com/

This web quest was created for a sixth-grade ancient civilizations social studies unit. It provides a teacher with a way to keep all his or her resources for a unit together in one place. The interaction is with the use of the website and the activities on it that were designed for learning about ancient Greece.

Provide the students with the links, video clips, resources, and assignments that they will need all at one convenient website. When links expire, they need to be updated, so they should be checked periodically. It will be used to teach the unit on ancient Greece. Parents may also find it useful to review what their child is learning in school by having access to the complete unit's contents.

The site contains images, videos, links (to information as well as interactives), and text. Each one of these elements appears in each section.

Standards Addressed

NYS Social Studies Standards

6.1 GEOGRAPHY OF THE EASTERN HEMISPHERE TODAY: The diverse geography of the Eastern Hemisphere has influenced human culture and settlement patterns in distinct ways. Human communities in the Eastern Hemisphere have adapted to or modified the physical environment. (Standard: 3: Theme: GEO)

6.5 COMPARATIVE CLASSICAL CIVILIZATIONS IN THE EASTERN HEMISPHERE: As complex societies and civilizations change over time, their political and economic structures evolve. A golden age may be indicated when there is an extended period of time that is peaceful, prosperous, and demonstrates great cultural achievements.

ELA Common Core Standards: Reading for Informational Text

RI.6.2. Determine a central idea of a text and how it is conveyed through particular details; provide a summary of the text distinct from personal opinions or judgments.

RI.6.3. Analyze in detail how a key individual, event, or idea is introduced, illustrated, and elaborated in a text (e.g., through examples or anecdotes).

RI.6.7. Integrate information presented in different media or formats (e.g., visually, quantitatively) as well as in words to develop a coherent understanding of a topic or issue.

ELA Common Core Standards: Writing

W.6.2. Write informative/explanatory texts to examine a topic and convey ideas, concepts, and information through the selection, organization, and analysis of relevant content.

W.6.3. Write narratives to develop real or imagined experiences or events using effective technique, relevant descriptive details, and well-structured event sequences.

W.6.4. Produce clear and coherent writing in which the development, organization, and style are appropriate to task, purpose, and audience.

W.6.6. Use technology, including the Internet, to produce and publish writing as well as to interact and collaborate with others; demonstrate sufficient command of keyboarding skills to type a minimum of three pages in a single sitting.

W.6.7. Conduct short research projects to answer a question, drawing on several sources and refocusing the inquiry when appropriate.

Visit the "Cradle of Western Civilization: Ancient Greece Web Quest" link: http://ancientgreecequest.weebly.com/.

Figure 7.2. The Cradle of Western Civilization

AMERICAN REVOLUTION: WEB QUEST
KEITH FISHER
http://sws5thwebquest.weebly.com/

This web quest was created for a fifth-grade thematic unit to supplement the classroom instruction of the thematic unit and is aligned with the Common Core Standards. It is designed as a classic web quest and acquaints students with the elements, tasks, process, and evaluation of a web quest.

It provides students with stops along a time travel journey, as well as biographical information about historical figures of the time period. Vocabulary is also included, so students can familiarize themselves with key historical terminology. Students time travel the internet and record their observations on provided worksheets to complete their journey.

Learning Standards Addressed

NYS Social Studies Standards

NY.1. History of the United States and New York: Students will use a variety of intellectual skills to demonstrate their understanding of major ideas, eras, themes, developments, and turning points in the history of the United States and New York.

1.4. The skills of historical analysis include the ability to: explain the significance of historical evidence; weigh the importance, reliability, and validity of evidence; understand the concept of multiple causation; understand the importance of changing and competing interpretations of different historical developments.

ELA Common Core Standards: Reading for Informational Text

RI.6.2. Determine a central idea of a text and how it is conveyed through particular details; provide a summary of the text distinct from personal opinions or judgments.

RI.6.3. Analyze in detail how a key individual, event, or idea is introduced, illustrated, and elaborated in a text (e.g., through examples or anecdotes).

RI.6.7. Integrate information presented in different media or formats (e.g., visually, quantitatively) as well as in words to develop a coherent understanding of a topic or issue.

ELA Common Core Standards: Writing

W.6.2. Write informative/explanatory texts to examine a topic and convey ideas, concepts, and information through the selection, organization, and analysis of relevant content.

W.6.3. Write narratives to develop real or imagined experiences or events using effective technique, relevant descriptive details, and well-structured event sequences.

Visit the "American Revolution Web Quest" link: http://sws5thwebquest.weebly.com/.

Figure 7.3.   American Revolution Web Quest

A TRIP TO THE AQUARIUM QR CODE SCAVENGER HUNT MATH CHALLENGE
MICHELLE CATANIA, NATALIE CIMINERA, DENISE REDFERN, CASSIDY RICHARDS, AND ALEXANDRA RINCK

This activity provides the opportunity for third-grade students to go on a physical and virtual scavenger hunt. The teacher uses the "instructions" code to start the lesson, after he or she places the "Quiz Questions" around the school. Each of the QR codes is a text file. There is no need for the mobile devices to connect to the internet to decode them. During this activity, students will read the *School Trip to the Aquarium* story together (https://www.readworks.org/article/A-School-Trip-to-the-Aquarium/719598be-f244-4c28-85bd-96500e5b71be#!articleTab:content/); students discuss the story and then are given "tickets" to the aquarium. The students walk around the school in small cooperative groups to find QR codes. Next, they scan these with an iPad with a QR code scanner app, such as QR Code Reader, installed. By doing this activity, they discover math questions relating multiplication and division to an aquarium theme and then record their answers on their Scavenger Hunt at the Aquarium Worksheet.

Standards Addressed

Math Objectives and Common Core Standard: NY-3.NF. 1
Domain: Operations and Algebraic Thinking
Cluster: Multiply and divide within 100
Standard: Fluently multiply and divide within 100, using strategies such as the relationship between multiplication and division (e.g., knowing that $8 \times 5 = 40$, one knows that $40 / 5 = 8$) or properties of operations. By the end of Grade 3, know from memory all products of two one-digit numbers.

The "QR Code Scavenger Hunt Math Challenge: A Trip to the Aquarium" can be found by going to the link: http://www.classtools.net/QR/qr_generator.php?fold=11&fname=7P5bF&diff=0.

The correct answers for this quiz can be found here: http://www.classtools.net/QR/questions_list.php?fold=11&fname=7P5bF&stage=&diff=0.

ECOSYSTEMS: BIOMES AROUND THE WORLD
LAUREN SPOTKOV

The following three activities address ecosystems, with the science one being first. Biomes of the World are represented in Figure 7.5. Biomes are part of our Earth's ecosystem as they are a community of plants and animals that have common characteristics for the environment in which they exist. With a partner, use the World Biome World Map to color in the different biome areas.

The color code is oceans—dark blue; wetlands—light blue; temperate forests—light green; tropical forests—dark green; mountains—purple; grasslands—yellow; deserts—red; polar regions—white. You may need the internet to check your answers. Once done, see if you can think of a way to conduct a role-play of the biome you select.

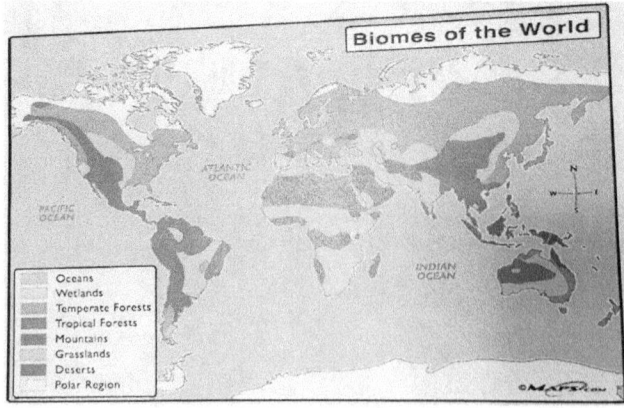

Figure 7.5.   Biomes Around the World

ECOSYSTEMS ON STAGE
LAUREN SPOTKOV

Here's an opportunity to be highly creative! The directions are as follows: Look at the information about different Earth ecosystems that are presented later in this activity. Convert each one into an information card. Figure 7.6 shows the information for grassland, mountain, and desert ecosystems. Next, working in small groups, select one ecosystem information card. Read the description and make clay models of this area with plants and animals in it. Then, put the figures on display on a tabletop. Finally, make up a skit about that ecosystem for the class to enjoy. Use your diorama as part of the play if you wish. Get more information about these ecosystems using the internet.

Ecosystems Information Cards

Saltwater: This area has average temperatures of 75–80 degrees, thick grasses, algae, tropical fish, and huge turtles.

Freshwater: A variety of turtles live here, along with other mammals, such as raccoons, white-tailed deer, and beavers. These places are among the most productive ecosystems in the world, with an abundance of life and a wide diversity of microbes, plants, insects, amphibians, reptiles, birds, and fish.

Prairie: Ecologists consider this ecosystem part of the temperate grasslands, savannas, and shrublands biome. This region is based on similar temperate climates, moderate rainfall, and a composition of grasses, herbs, and shrubs, rather than trees, as the dominant vegetation type.

Forest: A large area covered chiefly with trees and undergrowth. Plants and animals coexist with each other in this varied tree-covered biome.

Rainforest: Walk through this beautiful place and look up to see a thick canopy of leaves. This warm, wet ecosystem can be found near the equator and has an abundance of life that includes fruit, seeds, leaves, and thousands of incredible animal species.

Coastal: Land and water are joined to create an environment with different structures, assortments, and flow of energy. Coastal ecosystems could be salt marshes, mangroves, wetlands, and bays. Each type of coastal ecosystem is home to many different plants and animals. Coastal ecosystems are sensitive to changes in the environment.

Arctic: This ecosystem experiences 24-hour periods of total darkness during the winter months and is covered in a blanket of ice and snow, but animals such as polar bears, seals, and walruses do not seem to mind a bit.

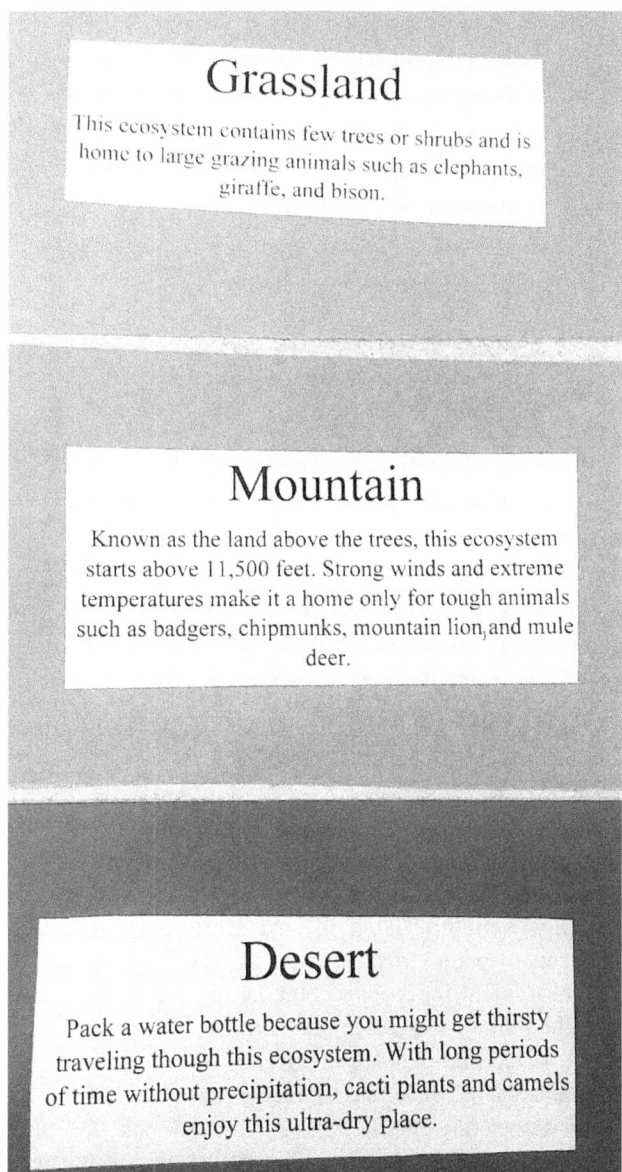

Figure 7.6. Ecosystem on Stage

ECOSYSTEM SCAVENGER HUNT
LAUREN SPOTKOV

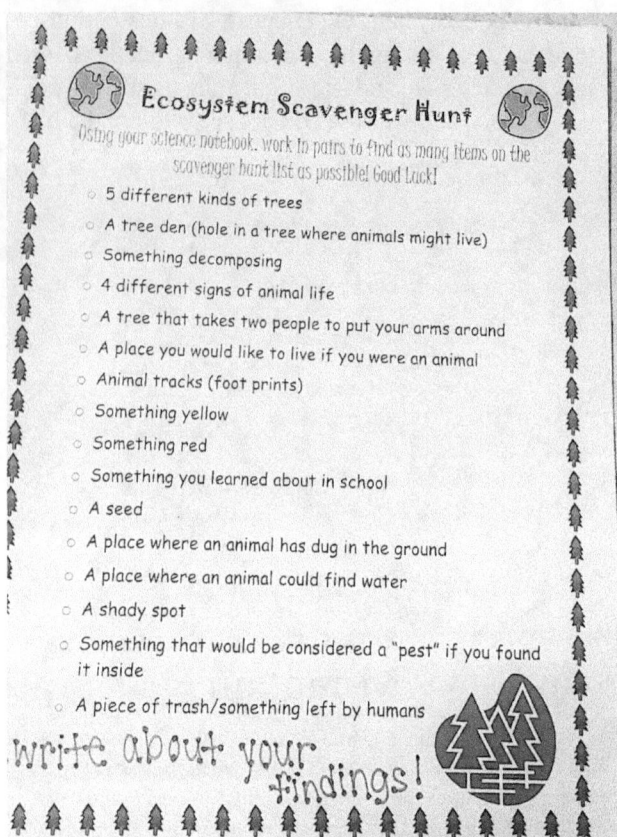

Figure 7.7. Ecosystem Scavenger Hunt

GEOMETRICAL SHAPES: LARGE AND SMALL
JENNIE MOORE

These next three activities are by Jennie Moore, who uses the math discipline for preschool children in her first two activities. English language arts is the subject area for the third activity. Using the math discipline, attention is given to geometrical shapes. As seen in Figure 7.8, you're to identify, by name, the large geometrical shape and then find its smaller counterpart. While the colors don't match and the size is different, you're looking for the same shape. Place the smaller geometrical shape next to the larger one and then see if you can make a design using that shape. Color it different colors and create a piece of modern art.

GEOMETRICAL SHAPE CLIP CARDS
JENNIE MOORE

In this multitask activity, you're to look at the large shape and then, using a paper clip or clothes pin as shown in Figure 7.9, find the smaller shape that matches the larger

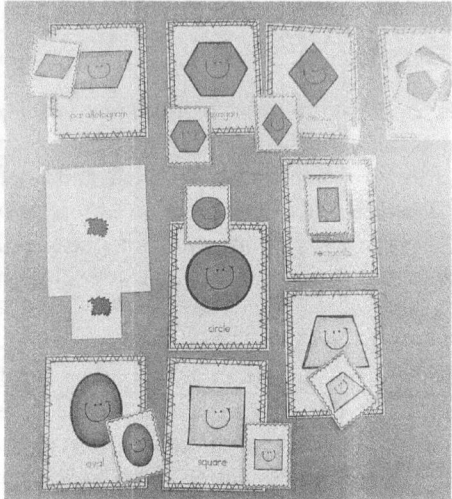

Figure 7.8. Geometrical Shapes: Large and Small

one. Six illustrations have been provided on the clip card picture in Figure 7.9. Your job is to recreate these six cards and then think of other shapes to put on a clip card. Perhaps you'd have a large tree and then a plant, dog, flower, and small tree as the choices. You'd clip the small tree. When making your clip cards, be sure to have the pictures be on the same topic.

Vary the position of the answer. Be imaginative. You could have a classroom desk for the large object and under it a chair, books, small desk, and bulletin board. The idea is to (1) name the main object, (2) name the objects under it, (3) say where they belong, and (4) know how the pictures of objects are related to one another—subject wise.

Figure 7.9. Geometrical Shape Clip Cards

KNOW YOUR ALPHABET
JENNIE MOORE

This activity is going to call for drawing the letters of the alphabet in their large and small format. You will need 26 shape cards for capital letters, and 26 shape cards for lowercase letters. The shape of the card could be a circle or square. Then again, maybe you want to make a butterfly shape, as shown in Figure 7.10. The card shape is up to you. Your job is to practice your fine motor skills and draw a capital letter and then lowercase letter on each of the cards. Be decorative; make the letters the same color but the design or colors around it different. If you're up to it, make a two-word sentence using the cards. Remember that each sentence begins with a capital letter.

Examples: Tom sat. I ate. Sit down. Come now.

Figure 7.10. Know Your Alphabet

GRAPH THOSE FISH
ALEXA LERMAN AND BRIANNE CATALANO

We read the children's book *The Rainbow Fish* by Marc Pfister. In this story, one fish, the Rainbow Fish, has very bright shiny scales. It looks different from the hundreds of other fish swimming around it. All of the other fish want to have shiny scales too. This main character winds up sharing his scales with the other fish.

These next three activities are about graphing, distinguishing shiny objects from dull ones, and then knowing cardinal and intermediate directions. Figure 7.11 has the graph and four fish figures on the far-left side. Note each one is a different shade. Working in a whole-class format, you'll need a graph template that is a large piece of poster board. Then, you'll need to construct a fish template that is 1 by 2 inches.

Everyone in the class makes fish in red, green, yellow, and orange. Of course, your class can decide on the color of the fish. Now, mix all the fish together and sort by color. Then, using the horizontal bar graph, graph how many fish you have of each color. You could use a bag of colored goldfish to do this activity, but then you'd miss the fun of making the fish illustrations. Think of another way to graph your answer. This could be a line or picture graph. You decide and make it for others in the class to enjoy.

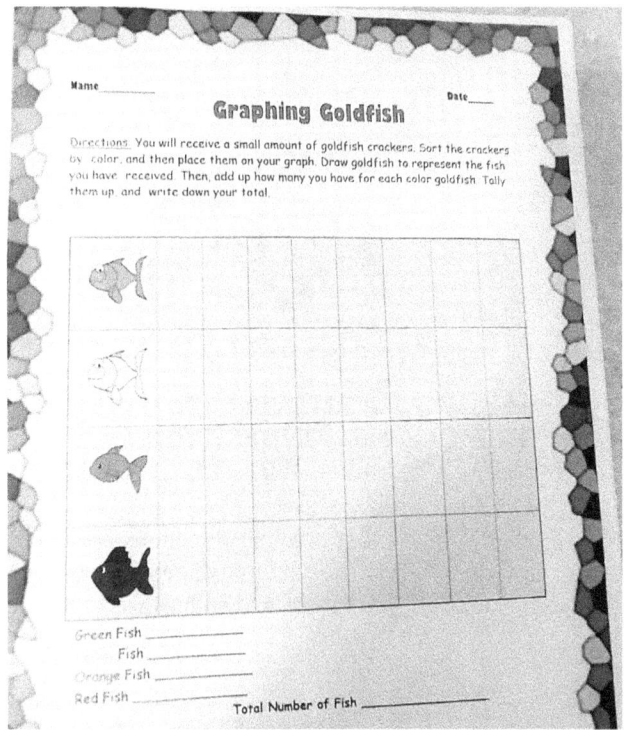

Figure 7.11. Graph Those Fish

SHINY OBJECTS FISH BOWL
ALEXA LERMAN AND BRIANNE CATALANO

Look at the objects under the fishbowl in Figure 7.12. These are *objects* that are shiny or not shiny. Working in small groups, your task is to copy these, then cut out the objects and decide which ones are shiny and go into the fishbowl. Place them there. Then, using your imagination, make other pictures of shiny and not shiny objects. Share these with another group to sort by the categories mentioned. Make a bulletin board collage or display for all to see. It might be titled "The Bright Things in Our Life."

Another idea about the topic of shiny objects is to form a group after you've done this activity and talk about the shiny things in your life. By this we mean events that were special, people that are dear to you, places you've gone that shine in your mind. Make pictures and either create a journal with these and a sentence or two about why they "shine" in your mind or construct a display board for an activity-based learning center.

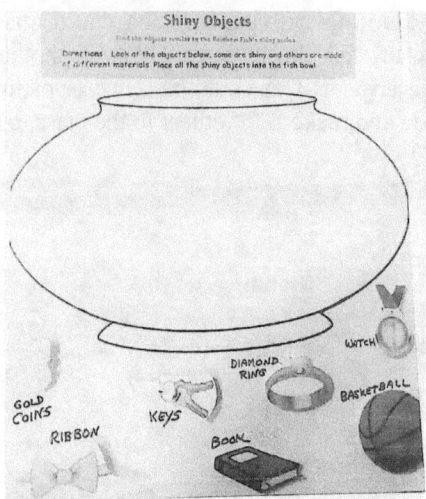

Figure 7.12. Shiny Objects Fish Bowl

CARDINAL AND INTERMEDIATE DIRECTIONS—UNDER THE SEA
BRIANNE CATALANO AND ALEXA LERMAN

You'll need to know that cardinal directions are north, south, east, and west and the intermediate directions are northeast, southeast, northwest, and southwest. In Figure 7.13, you'll need to look at the "under the sea" picture and see where the shark, crab, bright blue fish, eight-legged octopus, starfish, purple fish, orange fish, and jellyfish are located.

Sometimes there are more than one fish that's the same color, so you'll need to see if they are close together or where they are in order to answer the questions about their location. Please notice the colored fish have the beginning letter of their color near them to help you identify where they are. Fill in the blank under the ocean scene to play this game. Check with friends to see if you have the same answers. Make an under the sea scene of your own that has plants and animals in it. Write questions that have students using cardinal and intermediate directions to locate the plants and animals you have by name on the scene.

Now that you know cardinal and intermediate directions, write down in a notebook the route you take when going to different parts of your classroom. Walk the directions to the pencil sharpener, board, computers, and/or a friend's desk. As you do the walk, say in which direction you are moving. Now, take this one step further and do cardinal and intermediate directions for going home after school. See how well you know your way around your school or town!

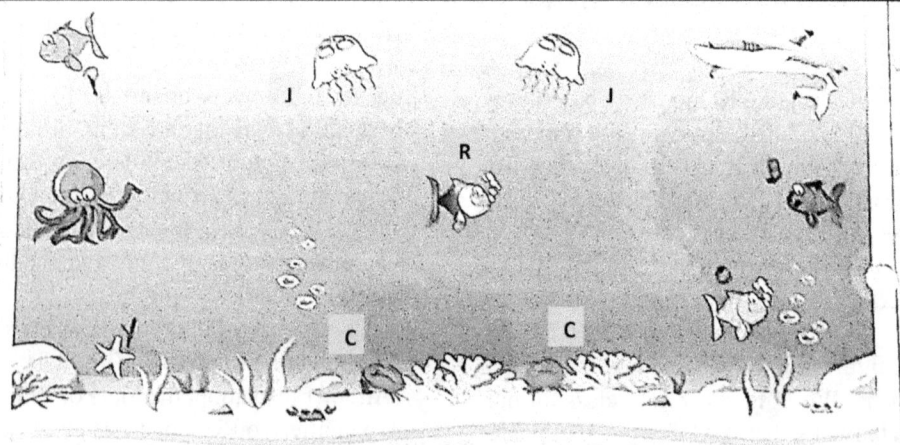

1. The Rainbow Fish swims _____ towards the friendly shark.
2. The Rainbow Fish swims _____ towards crabs.
3. The Rainbow Fish swims _____ towards blue fish.
4. The Rainbow Fish swims _____ towards the octopus.
5. The Rainbow Fish swims _____ towards yellow starfish
6. The Rainbow Fish swims _____ towards purple fish.
7. The Rainbow Fish swims _____ towards orange fish.
8. The Rainbow Fish swims _____ towards two jelly-fish.

Chapter Eight

Activity-Based Learning Center (ABLC)

Six Trifold Boards

This chapter is the result of an assignment in this author's 2017 freshmen Children's Literature Course (English 262). These are service learning projects that are designed and constructed by beginning college teacher candidates. When completed, they are given to local elementary schools as Activity-Based Learning Centers (ABLCs). A story map is in the center of the board and the outer left and right flaps have interactive removable educational games for the students to use/play at their desks. These boards are listed by the book title and names of those students who made them.

ABLC Figures

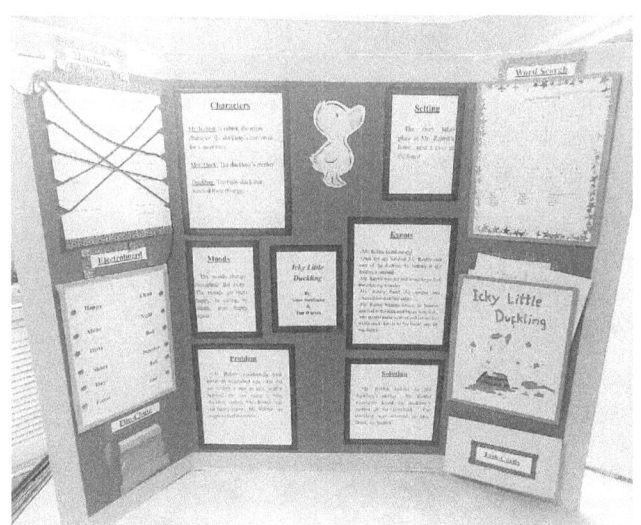

Figure 8.1. ABLC #1

Icky Little Duckling: Figure 8.1: Amanda Jilling, Amelia Morelli, Nicolette Pirrello, and Carmela Zampini

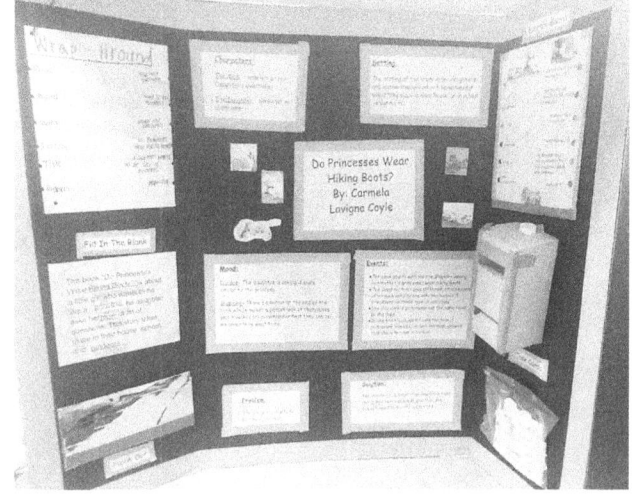

Figure 8.2. ABLC #2

The Other Side: Figure 8.2: Sarah Angela Danielle Cirillo, Stephanie Karalis, and Arlyne Mercado

Figure 8.3. ABLC #3

The Lion and the Mouse: Figure 8.3: Jake Gould, Chris Kelly, Alissa Leone, and Kate Loughran

Figure 8.4. ABLC #4

Rainbow Fish: Figure 8.4: Jacklyn Catalano, Gina Flynn, Sara Merkle, Alexandra Russo, and April Seera

Figure 8.6. ABLC #6

Hey Little Ant: Figure 8.6: Krystal Battone, Eileen Connolly, Kimberly Parker, and Emily Skupp

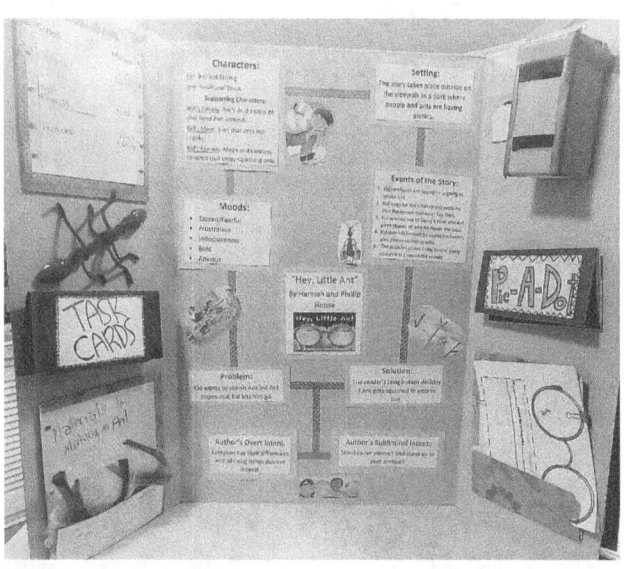

Figure 8.5. ABLC #5

Do Princesses Wear Hiking Boots? Figure 8.5: Lauren Habacker, Colette Holtzmacher, Samantha Strauber, and Sophia Valkiv

Chapter Nine

Graphic Organizers/Text Structures and Four Interactive Instructional Resources

Directions and Application

As seen in the previous chapters, there are a multitude of ways to differentiate instruction and have student engagement. This chapter provides several text structures for you to implement later. These, in years past and even now, have been referred to as *graphic organizers*. Subsequently, the terms *text structures* and *graphic organizers* are seen as being interchangeable. Their purpose is to facilitate different abilities learners' comprehension of grade-level curricula topics.

Instead of reading information and repeating it, the structures/organizers provide a means of shaping the information through the use of graphic design. There are six types of instructional differentiation explained in detail. The chapter closes with four specific interactive instructional resources with instructions for their construction and illustrations as well. Why? you ask. These are for you to use in your classroom or wherever you're engaged in assisting those with special needs and/or different learning abilities.

GRAPHIC ORGANIZERS/TEXT STRUCTURES: EXPLANATION WITH ILLUSTRATED EXAMPLES

Just for the sake of clarification, what is now referred to as *text structures* were called *graphic organizers* less than 10 years ago. *Both titles apply* and may be used interchangeably. But the former title is primarily used for this book. The use of this tool promotes student learners' decision-making, problem-solving, story creation and review, and sequencing, as well as character personality analysis and comprehension of cause and effect relationships.

Learners creating these "structures" or "organizers" address the thinking skills that were detailed in the chapter addressing the Reciprocal Thinking Phases (Chapter 2). What follows was originally published in 2011 (Schiering, Bogner, & Buli-Holmberg) and provides directions on the construction of the graphic organizers. However, most importantly, these tools provide an interdisciplinary opportunity to arrange/organize one's thinking for comprehension.

Text structures are designed to create visual stimuli for those constructing them or reading them for information gathering and clarification in a specified area of study. Generally, making one of these serves as a means for recording known information as well as speculative responses to specific categories represented within or on the organizer. And it also allows the student learner to construct new material with use of their imagination and critical thinking.

Text structures foster the use of creativity, reflection, conversation, risk taking, initial decision-making, synthesizing of material, prioritizing, and self-actuating for different ability and special needs students. This is to form solid inductive and deductive reasoning for present-time implementation. Additionally, applying this newly gained information for later subtle and informed addressing of life experiences is plausible. This would be the case whether the learners are in a social or academic setting. Most importantly, activities that are designed to develop, apply, and implement effective teaching are those that adhere to the needs of learners through this differentiated strategy.

Five of these text structures/graphic organizers are given attention on the following pages. Following purposes for each one of these, an illustration of each is provided.

The Story Map: Purpose and Illustration

The Story Map Graphic Organizer addresses a piece of literature's six story elements. These are the character(s), setting(s), mood(s), events, problem(s), and solution(s). Each one is addressed in a separate section of the organizer, with connecting lines to depict the linkages of story elements.

- The first section is Story Characters and should include the name of the character, as well as a personality trait and/or to whom the character is related or serves as protagonist or antagonist.
- The Setting section relates to where the story takes place and during what time period. This could be present day, in the past or future, or a specific year or time of day may be provided.
- The Mood section relates the different feelings the story evoked in the reader or those expressed by the characters in the story. They also may be what the author intended to inspire in the reader when specific events took place. Most importantly, moods in the story usually change as different events occur.
- The Events section provides, in chronological order, the key situations in the story. These involve descending actions, with the first one taken being placed at the top of the list and the last one being at the bottom of the list. Normally, these "events" are written in full sentences.
- The Problem and Solution sections address what the main character(s) had to consider as causing dismay, conflict, and/or confusion in that an action needed to be taken to alleviate the situation. These then lead to a culminating circumstance that resulted in solving this problem and the subsequent end of the story.

Story maps are used for noninformational books. And, overall, a story map provides the opportunity to analyze a story theme. The students may well learn about new situations that address thinking and feelings in social situations or academic ones, at home or in school. There is also an opportunity to reflect on what one might have done in a similar situation when the problem and solution are observed.

Interestingly, the story map may be used for "creating" a story as much as reviewing one. In this instance, the six elements are provided to give writing guidance and organization of thoughts, ideas, opinions, judgments, and feelings. This type of graphic organizer provides one with help making links from the characters to the setting, moods, events/rising and descending actions, which lead to the climax of the story/situation and result in a solution to a posed problem. The story map shows the following: characters' names with descriptions; settings list; what happened at a story's particular place or time; the

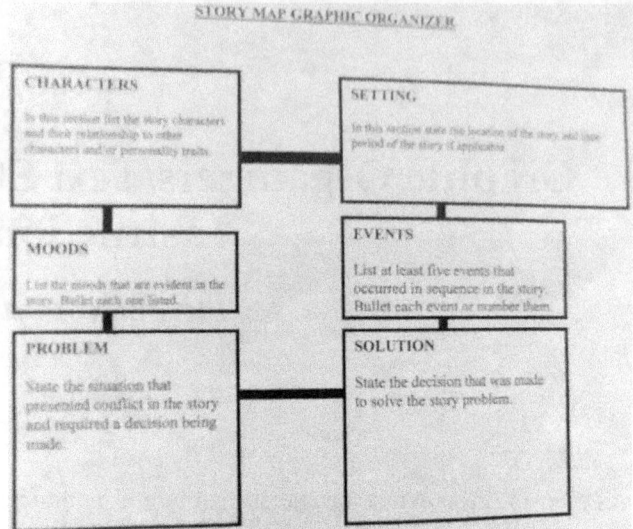

Figure 9.1. Story Map Graphic Organizer

mood(s), which are feelings characters experienced during the story; and the problem and solution as it/they occurred in the storyline with rising and descending action.

Sequence of Events: Purpose and Illustration

The main focus of this graphic organizer is to place, in order from beginning to end, what events occurred that were of particular relevance in a story, situation, projected encounter, and/or problem. The primary purpose is to illustrate the connection between one story's situational event leading to another one. Or the sequence of events may be a personal experience and just contain what led up to that ending moment without a final event or solution.

Construction of a Sequence of Events graphic organizer would be strips of paper with descriptive and sequenced statements, one under another, that could be cut out and placed on a poster board as follows: *First Event*: At age seven, I got on my training wheel–free bicycle with my dad standing by my side holding onto the back of the seat with his left hand. Dad said he'd hold on and run alongside the bicycle as I peddled and steered it; *Second/Next*: My dad held on as I peddled faster and faster; *Third/Then*: My dad let go of the bicycle and I noticed this; *Fourth Event*: I lost control of the bicycle and crashed into a curb; *Fifth/Last Event*: My dad came over and helped me get back on my bike to try riding one more time.

Cause and Effect: Purpose and Illustration

Cause and effect relationships are represented on this text structure. The requirements involve relating an action or decision to the effect it has on either the character(s) of a story, events, or the relationship of individuals in a real-life situation and/or imagined one. The cause and effect structure presents singular actions or dialogue with a short narrative.

This narrative has particular, dual, or multiple effects. These may be emotional effects, physical ones, or those that change beliefs and/or values. Then again, the relationship between the cause and effect may result in no immediate changes but much later, through reflection, show modifications in actions or words spoken. These effects will undoubtedly impact other causes and effects in the future. Imagine the Cause and Effect Graphic Organizer to be a chain of events with an explanation as to why each one happened. There may be a visual display of events if one chooses to have an illustrated organizer.

One of the most significant components and purposes of this type of text structure is that it provides an opportunity to make connections to real-life situations—common social and societal realities. This is accomplished while visualizing the scope and sequence of these events as well as the many possible influences of these on one's life actions, thoughts, ideas, opinions, judgements, or feelings. Figure 9.2 shows the cause and effect text structure.

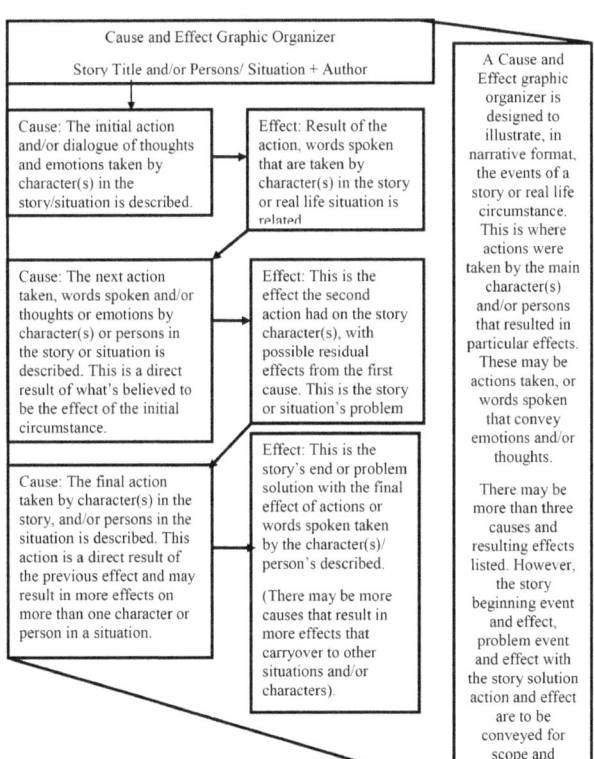

Figure 9.2. Cause and Effect

Character Analysis: Purpose and Illustration

Each character of a story, or person in our lives, has a specific role that forms the overall content theme of the story/our social reality with that person. The personality traits of each character are supported by events that occurred or dialogue that took place at specific times in a story or event in someone's life. Consider a book's story and the stories of our lives to be switchable, with only the characters being different or events being circumstantial.

The character analysis text structure lists personality traits and then supports these with events or dialogue with information that has been provided from the book or personal situations being addressed. While there are often several character traits, there may be more than one event to support each selected trait. One character trait is placed in a box and connected to one or several situations that verify that trait's being present in the represented story character/person in our life.

The purpose of this type of organizer is to involve the learner in reflection, analysis of discourse, evaluation of personality traits, making connections between actions and/or expressed thoughts and feelings, as well as to recognize, realize, and compare and contrast while synthesizing the story's action series.

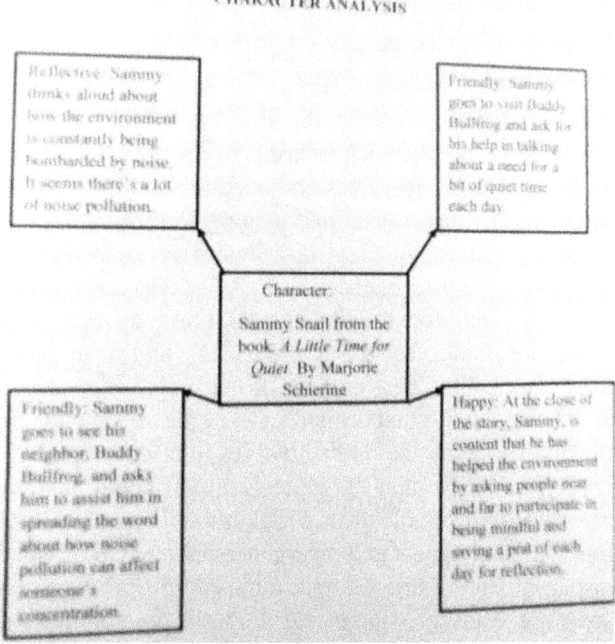

Figure 9.3. Character Analysis

Decision Making: Purpose and Illustration

From the time we're little and exploring things around us, we're involved in making decisions. However, our reflection on this process reveals that our decisions are frequently limited to two things. They are imposed, most often, by parents. Examples would be that we can wear sandals or sneakers, a green shirt or white one, go to visit a relative or friend, play one particular computer game or another, and the list could continue.

What's been established is a pattern of having two choices. This pattern carries over to the beginning and ensuing school years where the two choices may not be present at all because of teacher- or school-imposed rules and regulations. Or teacher schedules that relate exactly what's to be done at a given time on a given day in a particular manner results in fewer, if any, student decision-making opportunities. However, differentiated instruction through this structure's implementation eradicates that situation.

Provided for us in the classroom are the materials with which we'll work, whether we'll work alone or with another/others, the amount of time to do this assignment, where this will take place, and the specifications that lock it into a designed configuration. With this process, the ability to make decisions becomes clouded. In fact, this author suggests that an *inability* to make decisions becomes all too common.

The Decision-Making Graphic Organizer (DMGO) requires a statement of the problem or decision topic. Then, three or more choices are to be posed, with three possible positive and negative outcomes imagined and listed. These lead to a final decision, with reasons for this decision. A line is drawn from this choice to the Final Decision box. In that section of the graphic organizer, there is to be an explanation as to "why" that decision was made. The information needs to come from the sections of possible positives and negatives on the graphic organizer, as opposed to just making something up. It's important that the sections of the text structure be used to exemplify the final decision.

The student constructing the DMGO may choose to leave the Final Decision section blank and have classmates decide the best choice for the problem presented and the reason for that decision. Given the information on the text structure, they'd be involved in discussing which choice would be their "final decision." If doing this, the class becomes involved in decision making and reasoning, with convergent and divergent questions being asked or participants' suppositions examined. Overall, this text structure leads one to realize multiple possibilities for solutions to problems for everyday situations that require thinking and feelings' being evidenced.

At the onset, the purpose of this type of text structure/graphic organizer is to recognize the steps taken for one to make a decision within a piece of literature or personal circumstance. The problem and solution are related to those instances. The use of critical thinking is evident. Analysis of the decision-making process is heightened when analyzing *why* a particular decision was formulated. Children benefit from seeing this process's scope and sequence by examining their own thinking and feelings, as they prepare to make decisions. Applied comprehension is evident, with cognitive awareness leading to self-actualization; the highest level of metacognition.

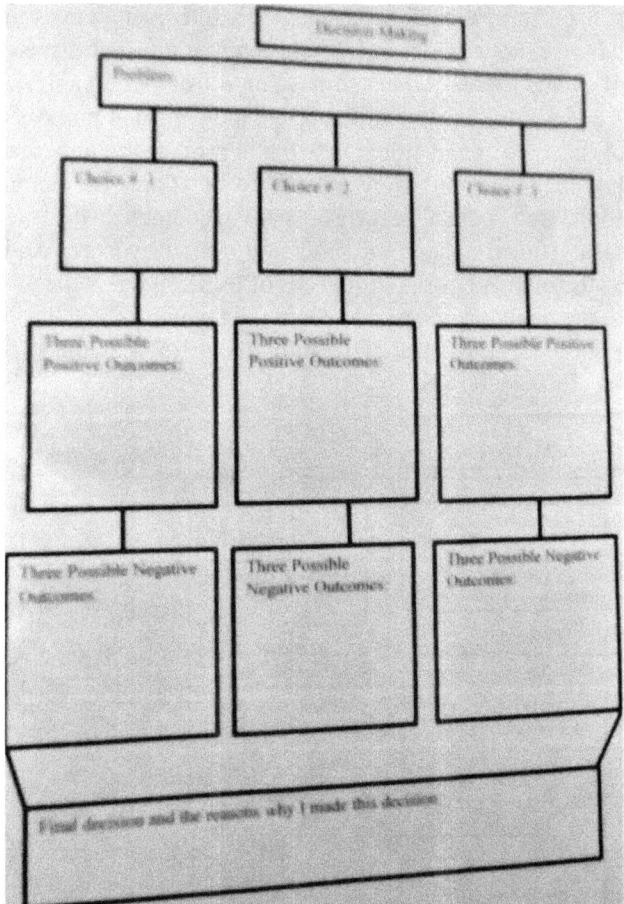

Figure 9.4. Decision-Making Graphic Organizer

Graphic Organizers/Text Structures 83

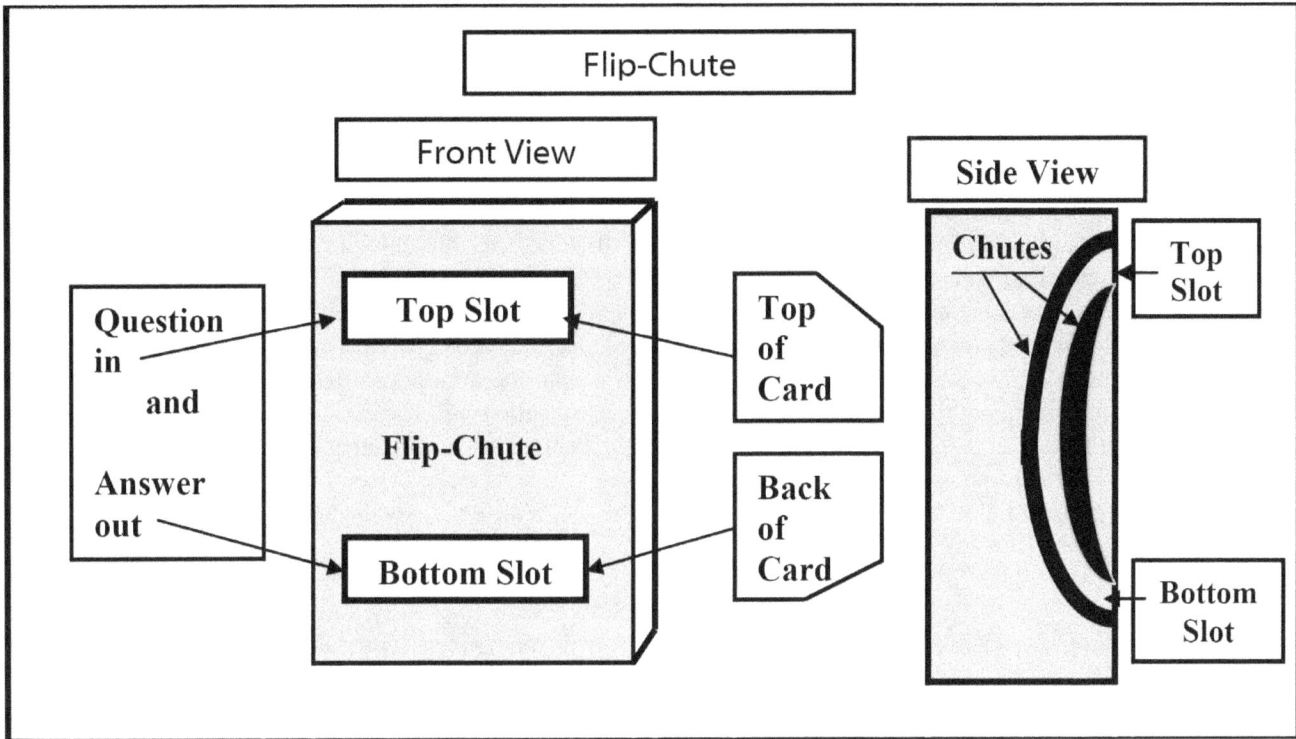

Figure 9.5. Flip-Chute Illustration

FOUR INTERACTIVE INSTRUCTIONAL RESOURCES: ILLUSTRATION, USES, AND CONSTRUCTION DIRECTIONS

Activity 1: Flip-Chute Holder and Cards: A Question In and Answer Out Activity

Flip-Chute Uses

This is one of the most often used and beneficial self-corrective interactive resources for tactile learners. This particular learning game is designed to assist students to glean information by placing a question/answer card in the top slot and receiving an answer in the bottom one, as the card flips over going through the chute. The upper right corner of the card is notched and this is where the question goes. When the card goes through the chute, the answer appears and one notices that the notch is in the bottom right side. That is because when the card was made, the answer was placed on the card by turning it upside down.

The student has control of this device. The learner determines when to let go of the flip-chute card, as the answer is said to oneself and the card goes through the chute. A pile of correct answer cards is made, as well as one of incorrect answers, with the latter being revisited until mastery is achieved. This learning device is appropriate for all age/grade levels. College students have been successful in learning foreign-language vocabulary,

Figure 9.6. Fish Flip-Chute

while elementary students have found the flip-chute instrumental in learning their multiplication tables.

Suggestions for the flip-chute cards with answers on the flip side include vocabulary with definitions, fraction pictures like one quarter of a pie on one side and the fraction (¼) stated on the reverse side. Another use is identifying story characters and their quotations, cause and effect, and even fill in the blank for vocabulary or sentence structure, synonyms and antonyms, or parts of speech.

Another idea is to have a picture on the front/top side of the card with the word on the flip side. Or one might have consonant blends on one side with the word *clown* and the *cl* letters underlined with a picture of a clown on the flip side of the card. Figure 9.5 has an illustration of the flip-chute and Figure 9.6 shows a flip-chute designed and constructed by Alexa Lerman and Brianne Catalano when they worked as partners in EDU 506A in the spring semester of 2018.

Flip-Chute and Flip-Chute Card Materials

Half-gallon milk or juice container, two 5-by-8-inch index cards, 1-inch wide masking tape, ten 2-by-2½-inch cut index cards, razor cutter and/or X-ACTO knife or box cutter, scissors, 12-inch ruler, contact paper, and thematic stickers for container decoration.

Flip-Chute and Flip-Chute Card Construction Directions

1. Pull open the top of the milk or juice container.
2. Cut the side fold of the top portion down to the top of the container.
3. On the front face, measure down from the top 1½ inches and then 2½ inches and draw a horizontal line that is ¼ inch in from each side.
4. Cut out that opening with the box cutter (or razor knife or X-ACTO knife), and repeat the same procedure at the bottom on the container.
5. Using your 5-by-8-inch index cards, measure one 6½ inches long by 3½ inches wide, and using the other card, measure 7½ inches long by 3½ inches wide, and then cut out these pieces.
6. Score the longer card ½ inch up from the bottom and the shorter card ½ inch up from the bottom and ½ inch down from the top.
7. Insert the smaller strip into the lower opening and attach it with masking tape to the upper part of the lower opening and lower part of the upper opening. It should form a backward letter *c* if one is looking at it from the side.
8. Insert the longer strip with the scored part going over the lower part of the bottom opening and tape this. The upper portion of the strip is taped to the back of the container. At this point, you now have the chutes in place.
9. Using one of the 2-by-½-inch cut outs, put a notch in the upper right corner and write on the card a math equation, such as 2×2. Now turn the card upside down so the notch appears in the lower right corner and write the answer to the equation.
10. Place the flip-chute card into the upper slot of the flip-chute. This step is done by having the equation showing with the notch in the upper right corner of the card. The card will flip over once it's placed into the upper opening/chute, and the answer to the equation will appear in the bottom slot of the flip-chute. Make as many cards as you choose, and have students make these in any discipline.

With each student having his or her own set of cards and flip-chute, students may switch cards with a classmate to learn new material or review previously presented topics. Laminating the cards is recommended, as they'll last longer than those not laminated.

Activity 2: Pic-a-Dot: Select the Right Dot for the Answer: Holder and Cards

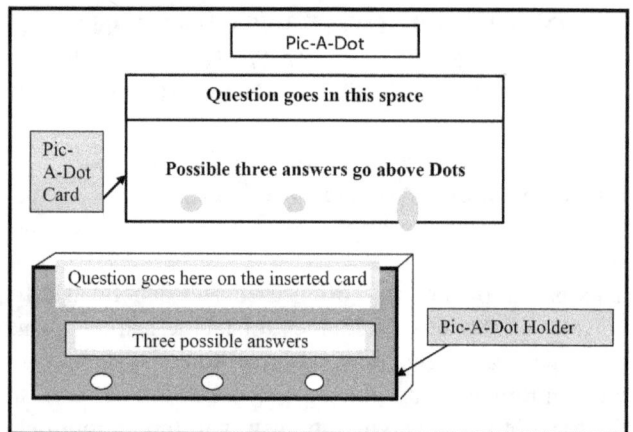

Figure 9.7. Pic-a-Dot Illustration

Pic-a-Dot Uses

This is a multiple-choice type of interactive self-corrective learning tool. A question or problem is posed, and then three answers are available. A pointed object, such as a pen or pencil point or golf tee, is placed in the opening of the selected answer. If the card slides out, then the answer is correct; if not, then another try is deemed necessary for this tactile game. The same types of uses as were mentioned for the flip-chute apply to this activity, with the difference mainly being the concept of three possible answers and students having to make a choice regarding the correct one. Laminating the pic-a-dot cards is recommended.

Pic-a-Dot Holder and Cards Materials

One 2-pocket folder, fifteen 5-by-8-inch index cards, one-hole hole punch, masking tape, 12-inch ruler, and scissors.

Pic-a-Dot Holder and Pic-a-Dot Cards Construction Directions

1. Using a two-pocket folder, cut this in half, vertically, down the center.
2. Choose one half of the folder, and place the other half off to the side.
3. Addressing the pocket, use your ruler to measure and mark ½ inch in from each side and 2½ inches down from the top of the pocket. Cut out this *U*-shaped section (see Figure 9.8 for visuals of areas to be cut out).
4. From the bottom of the pocket, measure and mark upward 1 inch and 2 inches and ½ inch in from each side. Cut out this rectangle.
5. On the bottom strip of the pocket, punch one hole on the left, middle, and right side.
6. Place one 5-by-8-inch index card in the pocket. Trace the top opening outline and each of the hole-punch circles.
7. Remove the index card from the pocket and punch the holes out. But where you will place the correct answer, punch the hole out all the way to the bottom of the card. (This is the pic-a-dot holder).
8. Place the index card back in the folder. In the outlined open space at the top, write a question. Example: The boy had two apples that cost one dollar each. He bought an additional five apples the first day and two the second day. How much did he spend on apples in all?
9. Just above the hole-punch areas, write three answers. Example: $3.50, $5.00, $7.00.
10. Insert a pencil or pen point into the hole that has the correct answer and pull the top of the card. If it easily slides out, then the correct answer has been selected.
11. Make as many pic-a-dot cards as you choose, and have students make these in any discipline. With each student having his or her own pic-a-dot holder and cards, students may switch cards with a classmate to learn new material or review previously presented topics.

Activity 3: Math Wraparound: Matching Questions and Answers

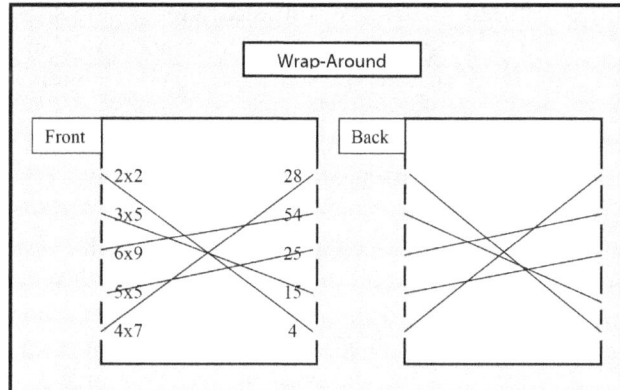

Figure 9.8. Wraparound Illustration

Wraparound Uses

This tactile/kinesthetic self-corrective device is a matching game with questions on the left side on a poster weight or cardstock paper and answers on the right side. However, answers are not placed directly across from the questions or statements. The size of the paper may vary. This interactive resource may be used for vocabulary with definitions and for matching characters with their statements/quotes.

It may also address identifying parts of speech, noun-verb agreement, singular and plural verb forms, math equations and answers, math word problems involving multiple computation skills, English or another language's word opposites, colloquiums, or foreign-language vocabulary words with the other side being the English vocabulary words. Laminating the wraparound is recommended for cleanliness and durability.

Wraparound Materials

One piece of cardstock paper (8½ by 11 inches), scissors, 12-inch ruler, yarn (or string or ribbon) of a color contrasting with the paper, and dark-color marker.

Wraparound Construction Directions

1. Using a standard 12-inch ruler, create a 1-inch margin around the cardstock paper.
2. Place a topic title on the top margin, such as "English/Spanish Wraparound."

3. Select the vocabulary or other criteria for the left-hand side and make a notch on the outside edge next to this word.
4. Select the vocabulary word definition or the same word in another language or other criteria for the right-side "answer." Be sure the match is not directly across from the word or what you have on the left side.
5. Notch the cardstock paper on the outside edge of the right side.
6. Placing a hole at the top center of the cardstock paper, string a 3½-foot piece of yarn through this and knot at one end.
7. Swing the yarn behind board and into the first notch.
8. Put the yarn into the notch on the right side that provides the answer/match for the first notch on the left side. Make sure these are not directly across from each other. Swing the yarn around back, and go to the second notch on the left side, as the process is repeated.
9. When finished, trace the back of the cardstock where the yarn appears. Use a marker or pen to do this. Now, undo the wrap.
10. The students wrap the yarn, beginning with the first left notch, to the correct answer on the right side until the wraparound is completely wrapped. This is a self-corrective activity because the student turns the wraparound over and checks to see if the marked lines match where the yarn is located.

Activity 4: Electro-Boards: Making Connections

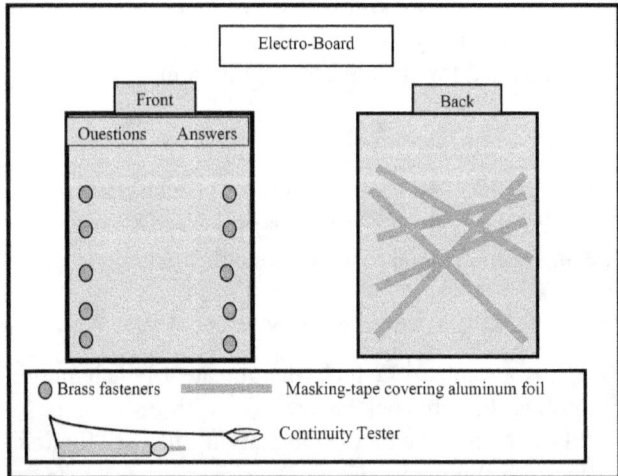

Figure 9.9. Electro-Board Illustration

Electro-Board Uses

This is a very popular self-corrective tactile and/or kinesthetic interactive instructional resource. It's kinesthetic when it's made poster-board size. One of the most interesting things is that these interactive instructional resources do not have a specified order for the match that's to be created. The connection between the question, such as a vocabulary word and its definition, may be anywhere on the electro-board.

Naming parts of an object, such as a flower, house, car, or animal, may have the part listed on the bottom of the board and a drawing of the object on the top portion. The student uses a light-type continuity tester and places one end on the question and the other on the thought-to-be answer. If the light glows, the correct answer has been selected, and if not then it's time to try again.

Such things as math problems in addition, subtraction, multiplication, and division; word format; English vocabulary and definitions; English words matching with objects or foreign-language words of the same object; Spanish or any other language/English vocabulary; identification of systems, such as respiratory and circulatory; or sequences of events, such as life cycle of a butterfly or frog or stages of human development might be topics for the electro-board.

Electro-Board Materials

Poster board, colored markers, aluminum foil, hole punch, ¾-inch masking tape, continuity tester, and scissors.

Electro-Board Construction Directions

1. Begin with two pieces of poster board of exactly the same size and shape.
2. Section the left side of the poster board to correspond to the number of questions you will be asking. Section the right side similarly for the answers.
3. Using the hole punch, make one hole at the point where each question will appear on the left side of the poster board or randomly. Corresponding holes should be placed where the answers will appear.
4. Print the questions and answers on the poster board next to the punched holes. If you desire, a brass fastener may be placed in the punched holes, with the wings on the reverse side opened fully. Answers should not be directly across from the questions.
5. Turn the poster board over. Place a ¼-inch-wide strip of aluminum foil in a line, connecting a question with

the correct answer. The foil should begin at the hole for the question and end at the hole for the answer. Cover the foil strip with ¾-inch masking tape so that there is no foil (or brass fastener) exposed.

6. Using a light-style continuity tester purchased in a hardware or automotive store, check the circuit by touching the aluminum foil hole and/or the brass fastener with the clip on the question or whatever is on the left side of the electro-board. Then, place the pointed end of the continuity tester on the thought-to-be answer on the right side of the electro-board. If the light lights up, you've selected correctly.

CLOSING COMMENTS

This chapter was specifically designed to bring forth specific ways of applying differentiation of instruction. While these explanations and artifacts may be used as a guide in the classroom or at home, they are just that.

You're certainly invited to try these and use them in your educational endeavors, and I hope you'll find these interactive means of involving the students in their learning beneficial for the learner and you, as the teacher. As we teach we learn and vice versa.

Part III

PERSONAL COMMENTARIES ON SPECIAL NEEDS AND DIFFERENT ABILITIES AND CLOSING THOUGHTS

Chapter Ten

Personal Perspectives Regarding Parenting and/or Teaching Different Abilities and Special Needs Students

This chapter offers you, the reader, with a personal perspective/touch regarding what it may feel like to be a parent, teacher, or both of students with special needs or different abilities. Trish Eckhardt provides her perspective in a narrative titled "Perspectives on a Learner's Dyslexia," which concerns her child's dyslexia learning experiences. Next is a narrative by parent and educator Tim Ryley. His contribution addresses having three daughters with very different abilities. This chapter closes with a commentary by Clare King, concerning her nine-year veteran special needs technology teaching.

Overall, there are purposes presented regarding recognizing, realizing, and identifying with your prioritizing of your instructional operatives/techniques from provided commentaries by the authors of this chapter.

PERSPECTIVES ON A LEARNER'S DYSLEXIA
PATRICIA N. ECKARDT, PHD

Introduction

When initially asked to contribute to this book, it was with the intent of providing a parent's perspective about my son with a learning difference. I attempted to write from the viewpoint of a mother with a dyslexic child. However, having been a teacher for eight years prior to becoming a parent, the perspectives of educator and mother became intertwined. This text examines the aforementioned struggle, discusses the trajectory of my son's academic and emotional growth, and provides recommendations based on personal experiences for teaching learners with dyslexia.

First Experience with Dyslexia

While I had taught children with learning differences in my elementary classrooms, I never understood the neurological component of dyslexia until I began my doctoral program, which focused on language, literacy, and learning. My initial exposure to differences between a dyslexic reader and typical reader occurred during my first course. I was fascinated by the findings of Shaywitz (2003) and the implications of fMRI (functional magnetic resonance imaging) images that revealed developmental dyslexia was a neurological deficit. According to Shaywitz and Shaywitz (2008):

> Extraordinary progress in functional brain imaging, primarily advances in functional magnetic resonance imaging, now allows scientists to understand the neural systems serving reading and how these systems differ in dyslexic readers. Scientists now speak of the neural signature of dyslexia, a singular achievement that for the first time has made what was previously a hidden disability now visible. (p. 1329)

Little did I know, years later I would begin to recognize characteristics of dyslexia in my child.

Our Journey

At the age of three, my son was diagnosed with a phonological processing disorder. He began receiving speech services for both articulation and phonological awareness. Numerous speech therapists, neurologists, and teachers assured me his delay was developmental and would be outgrown.

Specific reading disability, or dyslexia, is a phonological processing disorder that presents itself as an unexpected difficulty in reading. "Fluent reading—reading that is rapid, automatic, and with good intonation (prosody)—is very frequently affected, even in dyslexic readers who have learned to read accurately" (Shaywitz et al., 2017, p. 20). Twenty percent of the population are dyslexic; this equates to an alarming one in five individuals (Eide & Eide, 2011).

Although I did not expect my son to read at three years of age, his avoidance and lack of interest when listening to stories, coupled with the diagnosis of a phonological processing disorder, highlighted concerns. It was not until my son had the same teacher for two years, at the ages of four and five, that my observations were validated. Her 25 years of teaching experience, coupled with an innate ability to educate and understand the whole child, made her acutely aware of his different capabilities. These differences fostered growth as a family, as an educator myself, and most importantly, helped my child reflect and understand learning through a creative and metacognitive lens.

I have taught learners from kindergarten through graduate school. After completing my doctoral studies, I received training in the Orton-Gillingham approach geared specifically toward children with dyslexia. I co-founded a progressive elementary school where I served in the capacity of learning specialist and currently work as an assistant professor of education. This background information is provided *only* to emphasize the additional challenge, yet also strengths, of overlapping parent and teacher perspectives.

Since my son's learning disability classification, I have spent years struggling to find a balance between my roles as mother and educator. From a pedagogical standpoint, I understood what my child needed academically. However, knowing how to find a comfortable pace between home literacy and my son's disposition was one that needed to be discovered. A recent study in the *Journal of Pediatrics* revealed:

> The achievement gap between typical and dyslexic readers is evident as early as first grade, and this gap persists into adolescence. Identifying students at risk for dyslexia and then implementing effective reading programs as early as kindergarten or even preschool offers the potential to close the achievement gap. (Ferrer et al., 2015, p. 1125)

I worried incessantly. Driving to work, waking in the middle of the night, I questioned if my child was receiving proper services and if I was providing a sufficient amount of home support. I was concerned; my son was not yet reading or writing on grade level. Although he struggled academically, he was happy.

He was confident. My son was, and continues to be, supported socially, emotionally, and academically. Perseverance is a community value at my children's school. When academic struggles arise, teachers offer support by placing emphasis on grit and highlighting individual student strengths.

Recently, my son's resource room teacher spoke with me at his annual review meeting and stated, "He will learn to read. Let go." This statement was my turning point as a parent and as an educator. He is learning. He is reading. He is receiving the instruction he needs. He is happy. He is confident. He is learning at *his own pace*. Yes, he becomes frustrated. Yet he is proud of his accomplishments. It was at this moment that I found myself slightly letting go of a false sense of control that I thought I possessed.

Since I felt confident in his teachers' abilities to support him academically, I realized I needed to focus on my role as his mother, offering literacy support and emotional comfort at home. While learning differences present a tumultuous road for my son at times, our journey has continued to unite our family. This journey is what I reflect on, namely what led us to our current path and the academic growth my child has made thus far.

Early Signs and Parent Advocacy

When my son was an infant, he loved being held and smiled frequently. Always curious and communicative, he babbled and pointed with intention. When my child was a toddler, I often tried to hold his interest with picture books. However, he seemed disengaged. While I recognize every child is different, his two siblings approached text quite the opposite. I often fell asleep reading to them, as they never wanted me to put down a book.

At two-and-a-half years old, my son's speech was often unintelligible to individuals other than close family members. The *h* sound was substituted for most initial consonants; in turn, this impacted speech intelligibility at that time. Under the recommendation of my sister-in-law, a clinical psychologist, I contacted our local school district and requested an evaluation. These evaluations include a psychological evaluation and speech evaluation. Intelligence quotient (IQ) results placed him in the superior range; speech assessments indicated articulation and phonological delays.

Aware that dyslexia is a phonological processing disorder, I asked his speech teacher if she believed he might be dyslexic. She indicated it was too early to make such a claim. However, from that moment, I became aware of his differences. I reiterate here, this is *my* personal experience with dyslexia; concerns stemmed from parental intuition. Children are not typically diagnosed by formal evaluations until approximately seven years of age.

My son's daycare teacher also assured me his delay was developmental. However, this response did not resonate with me. We visited a neurologist, who indicated he needed to be around other children his age to improve articulation; she did not address the phonological aspect. It was not until kindergarten that his teacher, with approximately 25 years of experience, validated my concerns.

Her observations, coupled with a compilation of a neuropsychological evaluation at age five, educational evaluations conducted by the district, and an evaluation later conducted in second grade by the International Dyslexia Association of Long Island, validated a learning disability with characteristics of dyslexia and dysgraphia.

In kindergarten, my son exhibited great difficulty navigating and manipulating language. Although letter-sound association proved challenging, strong literal and inferential comprehension was exhibited. His teacher recognized his strengths in problem solving, analytical thinking, and strong leadership skills. My son's creativity and innovative ideas often inspired themes behind instructional centers in the classroom. Moreover, his school fostered project-based learning (PBL); creativity was celebrated and encouraged. *My child was defined by what he could do, rather than what he could not do.*

The three levels of learning consist of surface knowledge, deep learning, and transfer knowledge. PBL "requires that students have developed surface and deep knowledge in advance of being presented with the problem or project" (Fisher, Frey, & Quaglia, 2018, p. 125). Through the combination of direct instruction and constructivist approaches, teachers helped him establish strong foundational surface knowledge before moving on to PBL.

During his preschool years, the following characteristics were present:

- trouble learning common nursery rhymes, such as "Jack and Jill";
- difficulty learning (and remembering) the names of letters in the alphabet;
- seems unable to recognize letters in his/her own name;
- mispronounces familiar words; persistent "baby talk";
- doesn't recognize rhyming patterns like *cat*, *bat*, *rat*. (Shaywitz, 2003, p. 122)

As previously mentioned, when my son was a toddler, he frequently exhibited a lack of interest during a nightly read aloud. Perhaps his disengagement was an additional early indicator of a learning difference. Early signs of dyslexia for my child might also have included

- a disengagement with picture books during toddler years;
- diagnosis of phonological processing disorder.

Intervention

Early recognition and intervention are key to academic success. Beginning at three years of age, my child received speech services during the school year and summer months. Speech, occupational therapy, and individualized reading support were offered in kindergarten and first grade; he tested out of speech in second grade. In third grade, scores indicated my son achieved occupational therapy goals. Interventions during the early years proved pivotal for his academic success. When he was entering fourth grade, my son's individualized education plan (IEP) now included only one 60-minute session in the resource room daily.

Currently, my child receives small-group pull-out reading instruction, guided reading, and 30 minutes of nightly reading at home. He also remains at a school dedicated to a project-based and integrated learning curriculum. His resource room teacher is special education certified with a degree in literacy. She utilizes a compilation of multisensory reading programs and approaches that include, but are not limited to, Lindamood-Bell's Seeing Stars program, Phonographix, Orton-Gillingham, and guided reading.

Teachers meet weekly to discuss educational goals and appropriate instructional materials. As fourth grade comes to a close, it is clear that as a learner, my son has made the greatest strides in literacy achievement thus far. I attribute this to his perseverance, his teachers' support and guidance over the past years, a strong and collaborative educational team, and his personal developmental growth.

Now willing to read without argument, my son sees value and purpose in reading and writing. This year, and in years prior, his teachers maintained high expectations. They recognized areas of strength and honored his interests by providing opportunities for constructivist and experiential learning. My child's literacy skills of listening and speaking shine due to team-building projects and cooperative learning. At the end of third grade, an educational evaluation indicated his listening comprehension reached a seventh-grade reading level. I believe PBL and individualized small-group instruction facilitated learning.

Personal Definition of Literacy

My perception and personal definition of literacy evolved while on "our journey." Prior to becoming a teacher, I believed literacy solely entailed the process of reading and writing. During my early years teaching elementary classes, I recognized literacy also included the process of listening and speaking.

Now as an instructor of literacy methods classes, researcher, and mother of a child with learning differences, I define literacy as *a sociocultural construct intended to help individuals negotiate and navigate their local and global surroundings*. I often ask my undergraduate and graduate students to define literacy. As courses progress, we frequently find ourselves questioning and examining characteristics that constitute a literate individual.

Home Literacy Strategies

As both an educator and parent, I hope all learners are intrinsically motivated and driven by curiosity. Especially since home literacy is an influencing factor for academic achievement. I strive to foster opportunities for inquiry by allowing book choice, partner reading, and discussion about text. I have stopped reading for my son with the hope that he will continue to discover literacy's purpose.

Whether looking at a menu, reading cooking directions on a brownie box, or deciphering a weather alert on my phone, I know the onus now falls on him to try to read the material. Even when attending playdates, he is now responsible for writing letters to his teacher and bus driver alerting them to dismissal changes. My role is a guide; I offer support when needed.

Fisher and Frey highlight the importance of home literacy and contend that students who read 20 minutes daily are exposed to an average of 1,800,000 words per year and typically score within the 90th percentile on standardized tests (Fisher, 2018). Learners who read for an extra five minutes a day are exposed to an average of 282,000 words per year and score within the 50th percentile on standardized tests (Fisher, 2018). Students who engage in one minute of nightly reading are exposed to an average of 8,000 words per year and score within the 10th percentile on standardized tests (Fisher, 2018).

These statistics are an alarming reminder regarding home literacy's importance and impact. As a family, our aim is to consistently read 30 minutes each day. This has not been easy, as playdates, sports, and other commitments encompass our children's lives. We have made a conscious effort to prioritize literacy by reading during breakfast, reading in the car, reading before bed to relax, and making book discussions part of our daily discourse.

Before sitting down to read, I frequently heard myself speaking to my son and mandating, "We *have* to do our 30 minutes of nightly reading." However, this year I altered my use of language after reading Johnston (2004), who expressed his "initial interest was in how teachers' use of language might explain their students' success in becoming literate" (p. 2). Now, I often ask my son if he would like to read and express excitement stating, "We *get* to read together tonight!" This minor shift in word choice had an impact, for the better, on my son's willingness to read with me.

We often engage in partner reading and utilize echo and choral reading when appropriate. My son reads a page; I read the following page. When we began partner reading in September, my son read approximately one paragraph and his interest was held for a maximum of 15 minutes.

As we approach the end of the school year, we now read consistently for 30 minutes, and he can often be found reading one or two pages at a time. Decoding, fluency, and stamina all increased. When he begins to stumble over a word, I allow time to process, decode, and consider context clues. When appropriate, I intervene and say the word so as to not hinder comprehension. The purpose of my reading is to prevent fatigue and frustration, model fluency, and help with comprehension of text.

My son is currently intrigued by the I Survived series written by Lauren Tarshis. Reading books in a series provides a sense of predictability when he is engaged in a new text and enhances comprehension. After trial and error of different materials and genres, we simultaneously discovered his preference for informational texts and realistic fiction. These 30 minutes have now become our personal time; they allow us an opportunity to reconnect without distractions from daily life. I do admit, nightly reading can be a challenge. Although there are evenings when we are unable to read, we still continue to prioritize its importance.

Echo reading, choral reading, and partner reading are strategies that may be utilized at school and at home. All have proven successful with my son; they promote fluency, which is necessary for comprehension. Perhaps my son will become a fluent reader or perhaps he will not. Regardless, his grit and perseverance continue to strengthen through productive academic struggles; this is commendable.

Reflecting on high achievement in terms of academics, Duckworth commented,

> If you're just trying to get an A or an A−, just trying to make it to some threshold, and you're a really talented kid, you may do your homework in a few minutes, whereas other kids might take much longer. You get to a certain level of proficiency, and then you stop. So you actually work less hard. (Perkins-Gough, 2013, p. 2)

Duckworth's (2016) research suggests grit may be as essential, if not more important, than intelligence alone when achieving success. Great significance lies within this finding, because intelligence has often been perceived as the key to high achievement.

Discussion and Conclusion

Discussion

A teacher's and guardian's awareness of expectation theory is also a key factor to high achievement. Expectation theory occurs when teachers lessen standards for students; in turn, learners live up to these lower expectations (Sadker & Zittleman, 2016). Once a teacher or guardian reduces standards, a child might no longer feel compelled to work to his or her full potential.

Expectation theory perpetuates the achievement gap. In our household, and for my students, meeting high expectations is achieved through effort, work ethic, and analytical thinking. I expect my children and students to work thoughtfully and with diligence. As a parent and teacher, I strive to maintain high standards for all individuals regardless of differences. The following are key points I believe to be beneficial for both home and school practice:

From a Parent's Perspective

1. Set high and achievable expectations; recognize effort and perseverance over grades.
2. Acknowledge learning challenges; recognize that children learn at their own pace.
3. Read nightly. Engage in partner reading, echo reading, and choral reading.
4. Be mindful of word choice and language. "We have to read" versus "We get to read together!"
5. Find an activity or hobby in which your child is interested; highlight this strength and encourage the skill. However, avoid overscheduling your child and allow time for unstructured play. Play fosters creativity.

From an Educator's Perspective

1. Set high and achievable expectations; recognize effort and perseverance over grades.
2. Acknowledge learning challenges; recognize that children learn at their own pace.
3. Differentiate class lessons and homework; consider quality over quantity. For example, assign 2 quality math homework problems rather than 20.
4. Adapt assessments to meet the needs of the dyslexic reader. Assessments need not be identical for all students.
5. Provide visuals, prompts, and multisensory instruction for students with dyslexia.
6. Engage learners in authentic project-based and problem-based learning intended to spark inquiry and stimulate curiosity.
7. Use reading levels as a guide for instruction; avoid telling children their level. A level should be used as a teacher's tool to guide instruction; levels are not labels (Fountas & Pinnell, 2016).
8. Engage students in interactive read-aloud and audiobooks. A student with dyslexia must be exposed to developmentally appropriate texts to acquire grade-level comprehension skills and vocabulary. The EPIC app is a valuable resource.
9. Familiarize yourself with signs of dyslexia; document concerns. The Yale Center for Dyslexia and Creativity is a valuable online resource for teachers and guardians.
10. Integrate technology. We live in the most technologically advanced time in our history. Watch documentaries; listen to audiobooks. Explore current technologies for dyslexic readers.

Conclusion

While teachers and guardians may facilitate a learner's exposure to new knowledge, social and academic growth are complex learning tasks that require time. Regardless of differences, all students must be provided with opportunities to process information, make authentic connections, and progress to new developmental stages when *they* deem it appropriate.

My son's kindergarten teacher was a brilliant and intuitive educator. A month before her passing, she assured me he was going to be okay. She was correct; he has grown into a strong, compassionate, and intelligent individual. My child shares his gifts daily and has been one of my greatest teachers. Experiences as both an educator and as a mother solidified my belief that *children need to be allowed time to develop at their own pace.*

FROM THE HEART: HAVING DIFFERENT ABILITIES CHILDREN: THEIR DAD'S NARRATIVE
TIM RYLEY

Background: Our First Two Daughters

Our first two girls, born a few years apart, have attention deficit hyperactivity disorder (ADHD). As we were beginning our family in 2007, the first thing my wife and I noticed was that our daughter hit the "milestones" when other children did. But she had difficulty developing and maintaining language. Then there was her level of concentration, which was not on target. So we applied for early intervention by talking with her pediatrician and receiving a referral from him for testing. We went through that with the results being ADHD. Our girl received special education and speech services in preschool.

When she entered kindergarten, she had an IEP and was in a self-contained class. She needed assistance to stay focused, but she steadily improved and was placed in an integrated, cotaught class in second grade. That placement continues to this day.

We found that the coteaching situation has been helpful for "J," because she received differentiated instruction. The response to intervention (RTI) program was in place and she saw a pediatric neurologist. This individual provided guidance after a full neurological write-up was done and that impacted her learning experience in her classroom. Our next daughter, I would say, was the exact "same scenario."

The Third Child: "A" Was Different from Her Siblings

With our third child, while we may have anticipated ADHD again, we found things with her to be markedly different. There had come to exist, for my wife and me, a profound intuition as to what was right and what wasn't. This was based on, of course, our first two daughters. But also on what we observed regarding other children with whom our girls interacted. Also, the school situation, with what was expected in a particular grade level, played a role. But I am ahead of myself.

The first area of concern was that "A" was born early. Still, she was perfectly viable, and so we took a sigh of relief. However, there was a nagging feeling, a sense of concern, about her being six weeks premature. She spent two weeks in the neonatal intensive care unit (NICU). She was born with low muscle tone, and so she had physical therapy for a period of one year. This took place from the time she was 3 months old until she was 13 months old and walking on her own. We knew there might be some difficulties down the line, but we were happy that our third girl was prospering, eating well, responsive to us, and growing.

Around the age of 19 months, "A" seemed to be losing her ability to speak. It was actually an "overnight" sort of thing. Like from a thief in the night, her emerging language disappeared and her eye contact faded as we wondered what was happening. She too had early intervention like her sisters. A psychologist evaluated "A," and he said that, at the age of 21 months, she was too young to be diagnosed with autism, though she exhibited many of the signs of autism spectrum disorder.

With that evaluation, "A" began speech therapy and applied behavioral analysis (ABA) therapy simultaneously. Physical and occupational therapy resumed. It seemed like a "revolving door" of therapists in and out of our home. The county was very good about approving preschool services for our children. And our school district matched that once the girls reached kindergarten. It was one of those times where my wife and I thought, "More is better, as opposed to less." We wanted all the assistance we could get. And we got it.

Different from our first two daughters' difficulties, our third child's were far more profound. My wife did the legwork and deserves, in my opinion, a gold medal with her advocacy for our children. I am there for them, but when it came to researching our girls' problems, she was "in the know." This fact helped us tremendously, especially when we realized our "A" had autism.

By the time she was four years old, "A" had developed repetitive behaviors, self-stimulating behaviors like rocking, flapping arms, and so on, and she had become more withdrawn. Other issues arose. "A" went from being our "best eater" to being very picky about what she would eat. And her willingness to try new foods was minimal to nonexistent. We tried feeding therapy with mixed results.

In preschool, "A" was placed in a self-contained classroom where she received intervention services; different abilities equated with different ways to reach and guide her. ABA was now in place in school as well as in our home. Still, "A" has had a series of ups and downs in which she may gain some skills and then regress. We found that our third daughter has great difficulty with generalizing skills and retaining what she has learned.

Up to this point, what has been written relates to what happened, where the problems were, and what was done. There's another side to that. This is what my wife and I call the emotional response or reaction to our daughter—for her and for us. We were scared and worried when this all began. My wife and I would lie awake wondering, "Why is she regressing?" We felt that we were "losing her," as she seemed to withdraw more into her own world.

We know that we need to keep working at engaging "A" so that she is interacting with us as a family. As the intervention services were applied, we became cautiously optimistic that in time this daughter might be able to regain some of what she has lost. We are guarded, as there are no guarantees. We know that we love our children and that they matter beyond words to us.

Another thing worth mentioning is that perhaps we have more concern for "A" because her differences in learning are greater than those of our other children. In a condensed format, I think about "A" and her well-being for about 30 seconds of every minute of every day. Perhaps you need to be "in our shoes" to know what that means, and then again perhaps not. I can relate only to what it is for my wife and me and maybe other parents who have an autistic child.

Something not mentioned up to this point is that my wife and I are both educators. The impact that has had on our situation might be related this way:

- We are most aware of services needed for "A" to succeed in our present society.
- We want to give advice to other parents that it's important to investigate if you suspect something.

- Speak to doctors and teachers about what tests and protocols are necessary.
- Be willing to share your intuitive responses.
- Maintain an open-mindedness about how good things can be. Enjoy the happy moments and small successes of every day; in the long run, they'll matter more than anything else.

COMMENTARY: TEACHING SPECIAL EDUCATION TECHNOLOGY
CLARE KING

Allow me to introduce myself. I am a teacher. A little bit of my background includes my attending Molloy College and meeting the author of this book when she was the professor for a required English language arts and reading course I took. Years have transpired, and now I am currently employed by a school in District 75 (special education).

This school is part of the New York City Department of Education (NYCDOE). I have been a special education teacher of severely disabled students with autism for the past nine years. I have taught all content areas, including music, art, and, currently, technology/STEM (science, technology, engineering, and math). If you'd asked me back in my college years if this is where I'd be more than a decade later, I'd have not thought you correct.

I was drawn to special education because of a strong belief I have. This involves the concept of communication. I believe that every child can communicate. I also adhere to the idea that by using different modalities (auditory/hearing, visual/seeing, tactile/touching, kinesthetic/whole-body involvement) for designing instructional opportunities, learning occurs very agreeably.

And to add to that, I have seen, first-hand, how music and technology can engage every child. As an educator, I am always seeking new ways to reach every child who is placed in my care. I am always going for additional trainings to seek other ways to teach my students. Observing students involved in their learning through a type of instruction that engages them made me want to use this methodology.

The computers include the students visually. Then, there's auditory output and some input, when doable. And there is definitely hands-on involvement with moving screen objects here and there or following directions to manipulate what's on the screen. Kinesthetic interplay may not be readily observable as children are sitting at a table using the computer. However, whole-body movement may be part of an activity on the computer. Subsequently, there is the potential for this modality's being applicable.

Technology is an area of education that is rapidly growing and changing. This is a fact of home and school life. As a teacher in this field, I am continually going for training and certifications to keep up with the fast-changing world in which we're educating student learners. There are continually new websites, apps, and programs that help one to differentiate instruction and maintain a *running record/data collection* for each child and his or her response to the instruction, along with retention of it.

Overall, I love what I do because of the interaction and being a viable "part of now" when it comes to methodologies and the computer age. To see a child's smile when the concept one is trying to teach "clicks" in his or her mind is more rewarding than anything I could ever express in words. I know I'm doing something important and that there is pleasure with success realized by the students I instruct. Feeling good about oneself because of knowing about technology is special in itself. Specialness for special needs students with different abilities applied, constructively, throughout my career. This form of instruction is part of me, part of who I am, not just in school but everywhere, through heightened awareness of technology and its application to the population I teach.

Chapter Eleven

Author's Closing Thoughts

THE PRESENT

You've come to what's nearly the end of this book. At this juncture, you've had an opportunity to finitely discover the heart of this author's teaching methodology. And what has served as this author's motivation for writing is the hope that you, the reader, possibly a future or present teacher, will implement interactive teaching and learning strategies into your daily schedule. Remember, we are all teachers and learners of something, simultaneously, wherever we are.

As you've read through these pages, it is hoped that you've answered the questions asked throughout them. The reason for them was to have this book and the companion one, too, be as if we were having a conversation. For this author, writing in that fashion makes the book interesting and prone to being shared with others.

Those others, joining in a conversation about the Interactive Method's experiential strategies might provide more insight and techniques for realizing the following about what's addressed in this book: (1) means to educate all students, not just for the sake of educating or passing a test but (2) mainly for each one to enjoy learning, (3) creating memory, because the mode of instruction was agreeable to the student, (4) how learning techniques engage learners and are accomplished through differentiation to address the way students best learn, (5) provide narratives and accompanying illustrations of the IM's Interactive Book Report (IBR), Activity-Based Learning Centers (ABLCs), and Performance- and Project-Based Learning (P/PBL), and (6) elucidate the teaching of thinking using the IM.

One other thing this author brings forth now is the reiteration of having social cognition be such that the classroom is a place where students want to be, because of a sense of security there. How that happens, the past pages of this book relate, is through incorporation of teaching and learning strategies that bring about self-efficacy and self-reliance. This is partially accomplished through self-corrective interactive instructional resources and providing positive statements when a presentation is given or a performance demonstrated.

The main idea behind this author's educational philosophy is for learners to find self-satisfaction with using their abilities to realize self-acceptance. And one way of providing that for our students is having it for ourselves. Subsequently, our demeanor with those we encounter in the classroom, as well as elsewhere, requires us to be good role models.

THE PAST INFLUENCING THE PRESENT

In the late 1990s, this author's son addressed her St. John's University doctoral candidate class. He said, "You can only give to another that which you have first for yourself." So if you're negative with yourself, then that is how you'll likely be with others. But if you have self-respect and positivity, then you can give these to anyone.

Subsequently, this author presents the idea of imposing your "conscious will" to be affirmative with yourself and those you know. Then, you can experience not putting others down but lifting them up through your words and behaviors. One thing is for sure: *rely on yourself* to institute the methods and ideas for interactive learning in the classroom brought forth in this book and its companion one. You are the *change agent or promoter of different ways for different abilities*. You are the one on whom implementation of this book's content depends.

As an educator, this author believes our commonalities join us together, and there are more of those than differences when it comes to practicing our craft with interest and compassion.

In the 1980s, before book writing, this author was into writing verse about teaching and learning. The following poem addresses similarities of those in this education profession. This author hopes you have liked reading this book, enjoy the read of the following poem, and practice implementing instructional methods that bring about what these past 10 chapters have espoused.

Did You Know

Did you know?
I have been teaching for quite a few years,
And that I am concerned about my students' learning?

Did you know?
That I am brilliant in the classroom?

Did you know?
That I think about students' learning
Even when I'm not in school with them?

Were you aware?
That sometimes I think I'm smarter and/or less
Informed than others in my field?
I think that this depends on so much—
Like what teaching methods I use
Or *who* I am as a teacher and learner.

Did you know?
That I am basically a thoughtful person,
And like the willow tree I can bend?

Did you know?
Over the years I have developed
A comfortable level of tact and patience.

Did you know?
When I left college someone told me
I couldn't count on teaching being an exact science.
I've wondered if the knowledge of that truth
Caused me to, now and then, doubt myself.

Did you know?
I sometimes question if I'm successful
In meeting my students' needs.

Did you know?
I have taken graduate courses,
Post graduate courses, and
Professional Development classes.

Did you know?
I have been evaluated, staff-developed, and work-shopped.
I have been evaluated in each of the aforementioned.
I have been defined as disorganized and creative,
Or, somewhat structured and responsible.

Did you know?
This depends on who's doing the assessment.
I have been praised and also have not received recognition
When I thought a pat on the back was deserved.
Not so long ago I looked in the sky
And saw geese heading south.
I wanted to follow them,
And the next morning I didn't feel like teaching

Did you know?
I think I am in control of so much, so little,
So great, so small a task.
And, simultaneously, I think I am in control of nothing.

Did you know?
Someone who is not a colleague, but a person
Who matters to me
Said something that upset me the other day.
The person used finesse, but the words hurt.

Did you know?
I didn't think I was as effective in the classroom
On that day, and I felt disappointed in myself.

Did you know?
The very next afternoon
Two of my students commented on
How they like the "different ways" we learn.
This meant their being engaged in their lessons
And my not talking "at," but "with" them.

Did you know?
This was acknowledgment from students
About "How" I teach.

Did you know?
This is the meaning of Teaching for me.
My using differentiated instruction.
Sharing ideas with other educators
To create my own teaching style.

Did you know?
A fellow teacher came into my classroom today
And commented on how she liked the projects that
The students were doing.

Did you know?
She wanted to collaborate on ways to implement
These projects in her teaching and learning.
I had wings . . . I could fly.
I felt good.

Did you know?
I am brilliant in the classroom!
Did you know all these things?
Do you know me?
I AM YOU

—M. S. Schiering (1985, 2019)

References

Abedi, J., & O'Neil, H. F. (1996). Reliability and validity of a state metacognitive inventory: Potential for alternative assessment. *Journal of Educational Research, 89*(4), 234–245.

Abourafeh, D. (2018a). *One way does not fit all.* Unpublished manuscript, The Rebecca Center for Music Therapy, Molloy College, Rockville Centre, NY.

———. (2018b). *A phenomenological inquiry into an autistic adolescent's experience in relationship-based music therapy from the perspectives of the adolescent and parent.* Unpublished master's thesis. Molloy College, Rockville Centre, NY.

Amato, N., & Whitman, K. (2018). *Wrap-around addition: An IBR activity.* Integrated ELA and Reading, EDU 506A. Molloy College, Rockville Centre, NY.

———. (2018). *Does it melt? An IBR activity.* Integrated ELA and Reading, EDU 506A. Molloy College, Rockville Centre, NY.

Angela, S., Cirillo, D., Karalis, S., & Mercado, A. (2017). *An activity-based learning center (ABLC): A service learning project: The other side.* Children's Literature, ENG 262.02. Molloy College, Rockville Centre, NY.

Armstrong, T. (1995). *The myth of the A.D.D. child.* New York, NY: Penguin Random House.

———. (2010). *Neurodiversity: A concept whose time has come.* New York, NY: Random House. Retrieved from http://institute4learning.com

———. (2011). *The power of neurodiversity: Unleashing the advantages of your differently wired brain.* Cambridge, MA: DaCapo Lifelong/Perseus Books.

———. (2012). *Neurodiversity in the classroom.* Alexandria, VA: ASCD.

Astor, B., & Dodd, M. (2016). *Adjectives and nouns: An IBR activity.* Integrated ELA and Reading, EDU 506A. Molloy College, Rockville Centre, NY.

Baer, C., & Pearsall, R (2015). *Is it magnetic or not? An IBR activity.* Integrated ELA and Reading, EDU 506A. Molloy College, Rockville Centre, NY.

Battone, K., Connolly, E., Parker, K., & Skupp, E. (2018). *An activity-based learning center (ABLC): A service learning project: Hey little ant.* Children's Literature, ENG 262.02. Molloy College, Rockville Centre, NY.

Berna, S., & DeVito, A. (2018). *Perfect portion food groups: An IBR activity.* Integrated ELA and Reading, EDU 506A. Molloy College, Rockville Centre, NY.

Bernstein, K., & LeBlanc, M. (2016). *Wheel of adjectives: An IBR activity.* Integrated ELA and Reading, EDU 506A. Molloy College, Rockville Centre, NY.

Blair, M. (2018). *Disabilities, differences and diversity.* Molloy College, Rockville Centre, NY.

Bodrova, E., & Leong, D. (2007). *Tools of the mind: The Vygotskian approach to early childhood education* (2nd ed.). Upper Saddle River, NJ: Pearson.

Bogner, D. (2011). Tasks for the teacher . . . In M. S. Schiering, D. Bogner, and J. Buli-Holmberg, *Teaching and learning: A model for academic and social cognition.* Lanham, MD: Rowman & Littlefield.

Bogner, D., & Schiering, M. (2007). *Definition of feelings as "root responses" to stimuli.* Rockville Centre, NY: Molloy College.

Bosch, M., & Dacunto, K. (2016). *Life cycle of a frog: An IBR activity.* Integrated ELA and Reading, EDU 506A. Molloy College, Rockville Centre, NY.

Brandt, R. (1999). Educators need to know about the human brain. *Phi Delta Kappan, 81*(3), 235–238.

Bruscia, K. E. (1987). *Improvisational models of music therapy.* Springfield, IL: Charles C Thomas.

Bushnell, W., & Esposito, J. (2016). *Rhyme weave-around: An IBR activity.* Integrated ELA and Reading, EDU 506A. Molloy College, Rockville Centre, NY.

Calder, M. (2018). *Thinking skills application.* Rhame Avenue School, East Rockaway, NY.

Carpente, J. (2016). Investigating the effectiveness of a developmental, individual difference, relationship-based (DIR) improvisational music therapy program on social communication for children with ASD. *Music Therapy Perspectives, 35*(2), 160–174.

Catalano, B., & Lerman, A. (2018). *Cardinal and intermediate directions: Under the sea: An IBR activity.* Integrated ELA and Reading: EDU 506A. Molloy College, Rockville Centre, NY.

Catalano, J., Fynn, G., Merkle, S., Russo, R., & Seera, A. (2018). *An activity-based learning center (ABLC): A service learning project: Rainbow fish*. Children's Literature, ENG 62.02. Molloy College, Rockville Centre, NY.

Catania, M., Ciminera, N., Redfern, D., Richards, C., & Rinck, A. (2018) *A trip to the aquarium: QR code scavenger hunt math challenge*. Retrieved from http://www.classtools.net/QR/qr_generator.php?fold=11&fname=7P5bF&diff=0

Cedrone, C. (2014; 2016). The cradle of civilization: Ancient Greece: A web quest: http://ancientgreecequest.weebly.com/. In *Teaching Critical and Creative Thinking: An Interactive Workbook*. Lanham, MD: Rowman & Littlefield.

Cillo, S., & Nadell, J. (2018a). *Count the kisses: An IBR activity*. Integrated ELA and Reading, EDU 506A. Molloy College, Rockville Centre, NY.

———. (2018b). *Word Scramble: An IBR activity*. Integrated ELA and Reading, EDU 506A. Molloy College, Rockville Centre, NY.

Common Core State Standards Initiative. (n.d.a) *English Language Arts Standards: Reading*. Retrieved from http://www.corestandards.org/ELA-Literacy/

———. (n.d.b) *English Language Arts Standards: Writing*. Retrieved from http://www.corestandards.org/ELA-Literacy/

Cooper, C., & Molano, M. (2016). *Double digit delight: An IBR activity*. Integrated ELA and Reading, EDU 506A. Molloy College, Rockville Centre, NY.

Correa, A., & Kaiser, E. (2016a). *Addition number picture puzzle: An IBR activity*. Integrated ELA and Reading, EDU 506A. Molloy College, Rockville Centre, NY.

———. (2016b). *Roll a sight word: An IBR activity*. Integrated ELA and Reading, EDU 506A. Molloy College, Rockville Centre, NY.

Cox, T., & Malinowski, S. (2018a). *Know your weather: An identifying types of weather IBR activity*. Integrated ELA and Reading, EDU 506A. Molloy College, Rockville Centre, NY.

———. (2018b). *Let's look at the future you: An IBR activity*. Integrated ELA and Reading, EDU 506A. Molloy College, Rockville Centre, NY.

Craig, M. (2018a). *Puzzle tower our way to learning: Using "Jenga" for higher or lower order thinking*. Molloy College, Rockville Centre, NY.

———. (2018b). Who is the philosopher? In Foundations of Education [Academic course]. Molloy College, Rockville Centre, NY.

Crapo, K., & Sciacca, M. (2015). *Fraction action: An IBR activity*. Integrated ELA and Reading, EDU 506A. Molloy College, Rockville Centre, NY.

Cronolly, M., & Lessin, S. (2018). *Character heads-up: An IBR activity*. Integrated ELA and Reading, EDU 506A. Molloy College, Rockville Centre, NY.

Dacunto, K., & Bosch, M. (2016). *Tropical rainforest flip book: An IBR Activity*. Integrated ELA and Reading, EDU 506A. Molloy College, Rockville Centre, NY.

Dale, E. (1946). *Audiovisual methods in teaching*: Cone of Experience. New York: Dryden Press.

D'Antonio, C. (2017). *Synonym and Antonym Match*. Maple Road School 36, West Milford, NY.

Deaf Linx. (2018). Retrieved from https://deaflinx.com

Delialioglu, O., & Yildirim, Z. (2012). Students' perceptions on effective dimensions of interactive learning in a blended learning environment. *Journal of Educational Technology and Society, 10*(2), 133–146.

Dewey, J. (1945). Self-realization as the moral ideal. In *John Dewey: The early works, 1882–1924*. (Vol. 4; p. 50). Carbondale, IL: Southern Illinois Pres.

Duckworth, A. (2016). *Grit: The power and passion of perseverance*. New York, NY: Scribner.

Dunn R. (1990). *Rita Dunn Answers Questions on Learning Styles*. Association for Supervision and Curriculum Development, 15–18.

———. (1995). *Possible behavioral characteristics of special needs students*. St. John's University Doctoral Program, Sparkill, NY.

———. (1996). *Making interactive instructional resources*. St. John's University Doctoral Program, Sparkhill, NY.

Dunn R., & Dunn, K. (1976–present). *The Dunn and Dunn learning style model*. Englewood Cliffs, NJ: Prentice Hall.

———. (1978). *Teaching students through their learning styles: A practical approach*. Englewood Cliffs, NJ: Prentice Hall.

Eide, B., & Eide, F. (2011). *The dyslexic advantage: Unlocking the hidden potential of the dyslexic brain*. New York, NY: Penguin.

Esposito, J., & Bushnell, W. (2017). *Where do I live? An IBR activity*. Integrated ELA and Reading, EDU 506A. Molloy College, Rockville Centre, NY.

Ferrer, E., Shaywitz, B., Holahan, J., Marchione, K., Michaels, R., & Shaywitz, S. (2015). Achievement gap in reading is present as early as first grade and persists through adolescence. *Journal of Pediatrics, 167*(5), 1121–1125.

Fischer, K. (2013; 2016). American Revolution: A web quest: http://sws5thwebquest.weebly.com/. In M. Schiering, *Teaching critical and creative thinking: An interactive workbook*. Lanham, MD: Rowman & Littlefield.

Fisher, D. (2018, April). *Making literacy visible*. PowerPoint presentation at the Long Island Association of Supervision and Curriculum Development Conference, Melville, NY.

Fisher, D., Frey, N., & Quaglia, R. (2018). *Engagement by design: Creating learning environments where students thrive*. Thousand Oaks, CA: Corwin.

Fountas, I., & Pinnell, G. (2016, September 29). A level is a teacher's tool, not a child's label [Blog post]. Retrieved from http://blog.fountasandpinnell.com/post/a-level-is-a-teacher-s-tool-not-a-child-s-label

Garcia, M. (2012). Creative cognition. *Brain World: Humanity's New Frontier, 3* (4).

Gavin, H. (2018). *Point of view: Elements of characterization*. (Master's thesis.) Molloy College, Rockville Centre, NY.

Gervase, B., & Geraghty, M. (2016). *Map section directions: An IBR activity*. Integrated ELA and Reading, EDU 506A. Molloy College, Rockville Centre, NY.

Glatthorn, A. (1995). *Developing the classroom curriculum: Developing a quality curriculum*. Alexandria, VA: ASCD.

Goddard, Y. L., Goddard, R. D., & Tschannen-Moran, M. (2007). A theoretical and empirical investigation of teacher collaboration for school improvement and student achievement in public elementary schools. *Teachers College Record, 109*, 877–896.

Gosken, D. (2018). ELA and Reading: EDU. 506A. Molloy College, Rockville Centre, NY.

Gould, J., Kelly, C., Leone, A., & Loughran, K. (2017). *An activity-based learning center (ABLC): A service learning project: The lion and the mouse*. Children's Literature, ENG 262.02. Molloy College, Rockville Centre, NY.

Greenspan, S. I., & Wieder, S. (2009). *Engaging autism: Using the floor time approach to help children relate, communicate, and think*. Cambridge, MA: Da Capo Press.

Groce, Nora E. (1985). *Everyone here spoke sign language*: Cambridge, MA: Harvard University Press.

Guizzo, J. (Fall, 2018). Flip Chute EDU 506A. Integrated ELA and Reading. Molloy College, Rockville Centre, NY.

Habacker, L., Holtzmacher, C., Strauber, S., & Valkiv, S. (2017). *An activity-based learning center (ABLC): A service learning project: Do princesses wear hiking books*. Children's Literature, ENG 262.02. Molloy College, Rockville Centre, NY.

Hammerschmitt, B., & Sepe, S. (2015). *Fact or Opinion? An IBR activity*. Integrated ELA and Reading, EDU 506A. Molloy College, Rockville Centre, NY.

Hoberman, M. (Fall, 2018). Adversity Defeated: Turn Your Struggles into Strengths. Grade Success Publishing. Monsey, New York.

———. (Spring, 2018). *A parent and educator's perspectives on a learner with dyslexia*. Unpublished manuscript.

Hopper, S. (2017). Effect of atomoxetine treatment on reading and phonological skills in children with dyslexia or attention-deficit/hyperactivity disorder and comorbid dyslexia in a randomized, placebo-controlled trial. *Journal of Child and Adolescent Psychopharmacology, 27*(1), 19–28. doi:10.1089/cap.2015.0189

Hunter, M. (1916–1994). In R. E. Salvin. (1989) "On mastery learning and mastery teaching." Alexandria, VA: ASCD.

Hunter, M. (1964). Retrieved from https://www.slideshare.net/stmns/copy-of-term-1-2018-parent-gifted-workshop-slides-90341559

Individuals with Disabilities Education Act. (2004). Part 300.8 (a) (1). Appendix F to part 300—index for IDEA—part B (34 CFR Part 300). National Institute of Child Health and Development (NICHD). Retrieved from https://sites.ed.gov/idea/regs/b/d/300.304/b/3

International Dyslexia Association. (2018). Retrieved from https://dyslexiaida.org/

International Society for Technology in Education. (2007). ISTE standards students. *ISTE Standards*. Retrieved from https://id.iste.org/docs/pdfs/20-14_ISTE_Standards-s_PDF.pdf

Jaarsma, P., & Welin, S. (2012). Autism as a natural human variation: Reflections on the claims of the neurodiversity movement. *Health Care Analysis, 20*(1), 20–30.

Jacoby, L. A. (1991). A process dissociation framework: Separating automatic from intentional uses of memory. *Journal of Memory and Language* 30, 513–541.

Jilling, A., Morelli, A., Pirrello, N., & Zampini, C. (2017). *An activity-based learning center (ABLC): A service learning project: Icky little duckling*. Children's Literature, ENG 262.02. Molloy College, Rockville Centre, NY.

Johnston, P. (2004). *Choice words: How language affects children's learning*. Portland, ME: Stenhouse.

Keefe, J. W. (Ed.). (1979). *Learning styles: An overview, the student learning styles: Diagnosing and prescribing programs* (pp. 1–17), Reston, VA: National Association of Secondary School Principals.

Keefe, J. W., & Languis, M. (1983). Description of the learning style profile. In J. W. Keefe and J. S. Monk (Eds.), *NASSP Bulletin* (pp. 43–53). Reston, VA: National Association of Secondary School Principals.

Kelly, M. (2017). Defining project and performance based learning. Retrieved from http://www.thoughtco.com

King, C. (2010). *Homes—yesterday and today: An IBR activity*. Integrated ELA and Reading, EDU 506A. Molloy College, Rockville Centre, NY.

———. (2018). *Commentary: Teaching special education technology: A narrative*. NYC District 75 (Special Education Technology), New York City, NY.

LaCasse, K., & Valente, D. (2018). *Who am I: Guess the planet: An IBR activity*. Integrated ELA and Reading, EDU 506A. Molloy College, Rockville Centre, NY.

Lane, R. (2018). *Biology: Food webs: Special education grades 7–12*. (Master's thesis.) Molloy College, Rockville Centre, NY.

Larkin, J. (2010b). *Communication: Braille: An IBR activity*. Integrated ELA and Reading, EDU 506A. Molloy College, Rockville Centre, NY.

———. (2010a). *Three-dimensional super word search: Geoboard: An IBR activity*. Integrated ELA and Reading, EDU 506A. Molloy College, Rockville Centre, NY.

Laupheimer, L. (2016). Enjoyment of interactive learning. In M. Schiering, *Learning and teaching creative cognition: The interactive book report*. Lanham, MD: Rowman & Littlefield.

LeBlanc, M., & Bernstein, K. (2016). *Butterfly flip-chute*: An IBR activity. Integrated ELA Reading, EDU 506A. Molloy College, Rockville Centre, NY.

Lerman, A., & Catalano, B. (2018a). *A fish flip-chute: An IBR activity*. Integrated ELA and Reading, EDU 506A. Molloy College, Rockville Centre, NY.

———. (2018b). *Graph those fish: An IBR activity*. Integrated ELA and Reading, EDU 506A. Molloy College, Rockville Centre, NY.

———. (2018c). *Shiny objects fish bowl: An IBR activity*. Integrated ELA and Reading, Course; EDU 506A. Molloy College, Rockville Centre, NY.

Lessin, S., & Cronolly, M. (2018). *Jumping through hoops: Compound words: An IBR activity*. Integrated ELA and Reading, EDU 506A. Molloy College, Rockville Centre, NY.

Lungaro, N. (2017). *Small, medium and large: A sorting by size activity*. ABA Preschool Class at Maple Road School 36, West Milford, NJ.

Maheshwari, V. K. (2016). Edgar Dale's Cone of Experience. Retrieved from http://www.vkmaheshwari.com/WP/?p=2332

Malinowski, S., & Cox, T. (2018). *Sequence of events story train: An IBR activity*. Integrated ELA and Reading, EDU 506A. Molloy College, Rockville Centre, NY.

Marmol, J., & McMahon Egan, B. (2016a). *Calendar creation: An IBR activity*. Integrated ELA and Reading, EDU 506A. Molloy College, Rockville Centre, NY.

———. (2016b). *Math/science temperature task cards: Fahrenheit and Celsius: An IBR activity*. Integrated ELA and Reading, EDU 506A. Molloy College, Rockville Centre, NY.

McMahon Egan, B., & Marmol, J. (2016). *Cloud making: An IBR activity*. Integrated ELA and Reading, EDU 506A. Molloy College, Rockville Centre, NY.

McTighe, J., & Wiggins, G. (1999). *Understanding by design professional development workbook*. Alexandria, VA: ASCD.

Minogue, A., & Murnane, M. (2016). *I can recycle: An IBR activity*. Integrated ELA and Reading, EDU 506A. Molloy College, Rockville Centre, NY.

Mlodinow, L. *The Genius Section: Unfreeze Your Brain*. December 2018/January 2019: Reader's Digest. New York: Pleasantville, 118–120.

Molano, M., & Cooper, C. (2016). *Dinosaur subtraction game*: *An IBR activity*. Integrated ELA and Reading, EDU 506A. Molloy College, Rockville Centre, NY.

Moore, J. (2014a). *Geometrical shapes: Large and small: An IBR activity*. Integrated ELA and Reading; EDU 506A. Molloy College, Rockville Center, NY.

———. (2014b). *Geometrical shape clip cards: An IBR activity*. Integrated ELA and Reading EDU 506A. Molloy College, Rockville Centre, NY.

———. (2014c). *Know your alphabet: An IBR activity*. Integrated ELA and Reading EDU 506A. Molloy College, Rockville Centre, NY.

———. (2014d). *Under-over sewing: An IBR activity*. Integrated Reading and ELA, EDU 506A. Molloy College, Rockville Centre, NY.

Moroney, R. (2016). *Long Island during the American Revolution: An e-textbook chapter*. In M. Schiering, *Teaching creative and critical thinking: An interactive workbook*. Lanham, MD: Rowman & Littlefield. Retrieved from http://revolutionarylongisland.weebly.com/

———. (2017). *Comments on receiving and interpreting information*. Division of Education, Molloy College, Rockville Centre, NY.

Murnane, M., & Minogue, A. (2017). *Earth day history: An IBR activity*. Integrated ELA and Reading, EDU 506A. Molloy College, Rockville Centre, NY.

Nadell, J. (2018). *Making a sentence: An IBR activity*. Integrated ELA and Reading, EDU 506A. Molloy College, Rockville Centre, NY.

National Center on Response to Intervention. (2018). Home page. Retrieved from www.rti4success.org

Nordoff, P., & Robbins, C. (2007). *Creative music therapy: A guide to fostering clinical musicianship* (2nd Ed.). Gilsum, NH: Barcelona.

Office of Higher Education, New York State Education Department. (n.d.). *Social Studies Standards*. Retrieved from http://www.highered.nysed.gov/kiap/precoll/service_learn/standards/ss.pdf

Olsen, D. G. (1995). "Less" can be "more" in the promotion of thinking. *Social Education, 59*(3), 130–138.

Paccione, M. (2018). *Fun with tallying and graphing: An interactive learning exercise*. Woodside School, River Vale, NJ.

Perkins-Gough, D. (2013). The significance of grit: A conversation with Angela Lee Duckworth. *Educational Leadership, 71*(1), 14–20.

Polirer, I., & Rocioppi, C. M. (2018a). *Character captions: An IBR activity*. Integrated ELA and Reading, EDU 506A. Molloy College, Rockville Centre, NY.

———. (2018b). *Pic-a-dot: Do it! An IBR activity*. Integrated ELA and Reading, EDU 506A. Molloy College, Rockville Centre, NY.

Raynor & Armstrong et al. (eds.). (2003). The "how" and "who" of teaching and learning. *Bridging Theory and Practice*. ELSIN 8th International European Learning Style Conference. Ghent, Belgium.

Reavis, G. (1940; 1999). *The animal school*. Peterborough, NH: Crystal Springs Books.

Redondo, J. (2018). Careers Path Options: My Five-Year Career Choice, Fireman, Teacher/Professor, Law Enforcement. Decision Making Graphic Organizer, Integrated ELA and Reading; EDU. 506A. Molloy College, Rockville Centre, NY.

Riba, N. (2018, unpublished). *Rotation of a geometric shape: A class assignment and idea for interactive learning of geometry*. New York, NY.

Robertson, S. M. (2009). Neurodiversity, quality of life, and autistic adults: Shifting research and professional focuses onto real-life challenges. *Disability Studies Quarterly, 30*(1).

RTI Action Network. (2018). *What is RTI?* Retrieved from www.rtinetwork.org/learn/what

Ryley, T. (2018). *From the heart: Having different abilities children: Their dad's narrative.* Baldwin Senior High School, Levittown, NY.

Sadker, D. M., & Zittleman, K. R. (2016). *Teachers, schools, and society: A brief introduction to education* (4th ed.). New York, NY: McGraw-Hill.

Schiering, J. (2017). *Special education: A resource room teachers views*. Manch Elementary School, Las Vegas, NV.

Schiering, M. S. (1996). *The classroom as a comfort zone*. Stony Point Elementary School, Stony Point, NY.

———. (1999). *The reciprocal thinking phases: Cognition and metacognition*. (Doctoral dissertation). St. John's University, Queens, NY; Molloy College. Rockville Centre, NY.

———. (2000–present). *NYS Project SAVE (safe schools against violence in education)* syllabus p. 14. Molloy College, Rockville Centre, NY.

———. (2014a). Character trait role-play. In *Teaching critical and creative thinking: An interactive workbook*. Lanham, MD: Rowman & Littlefield.

———. (2014b). *Dignity for all students act: NYS Teacher Certification Workshop*. PPT slide 36. Molloy College. Rockville Centre, NY.

Schiering, M. S. (2014; 2015). Qualities of a leader, from LinkedIn "Princess bride" leadership lessons. In M. S. Schiering, *Learning and teaching creative cognition: The interactive book report* (pp. 51–58). Lanham, MD: Rowman & Littlefield. Retrieved from https://www.linkedin.com/plus

———. (2015). *Learning and teaching creative cognition: The interactive book report.* Lanham, MD: Rowman & Littlefield, 40.

———. (2016a). Geometric shapes: A math word problem floor game. In *Teaching critical and creative thinking: An interactive workbook.* Lanham, MD: Rowman & Littlefield.

———. (2016b). *Teaching Creative and Critical Thinking: An Interactive Workbook.* Lanham, MD: Rowman & Littlefield.

———. (2017). *What's right with you: An interactive character development guide.* Lanham, MD. Rowman & Littlefield.

———. (2017–present). Eng. 262.02. Children's literature course syllabus. Molloy College. Rockville Centre, NY.

———. (2019). Self published. Stony Point, NY.

Schiering, M. S., & Bogner, D. (2008; 2011). Definitions of thoughts, ideas, opinions, judgments and feelings. In M. Schiering, D. Bogner, & J. Buli-Holmerg, *Teaching and learning: A model for academic and social cognition.* Lanham, MD: Rowman & Littlefield.

Schiering, M. S., Bogner, D., & Buli-Holmberg, J. (2011). *Teaching and Learning: A Model for Academic and Social Cognition.* Lanham, MD: Rowman & Littlefield, 106.

Schiering, M. S., & Marino, A. (2016). Thoughts on using the IBR and interactive instructional resources. In M. Schiering, *Teaching creative and critical thinking: An interactive workbook.* Lanham, MD: Rowman & Littlefield.

Schon, D. (1997). *Reflective practice and professional development.* Retrieved from http://eric.ed.gov/

Sepe, S., & Hammerschmitt, B. (2015). *Mobile of positives and goals: An IBR activity.* Integrated ELA and Reading, EDU 506A. Molloy College, Rockville Centre, NY.

Shaywitz, S. (2003). *Overcoming dyslexia: A new and complete science-based program for reading problems at any level.* New York, NY: Vintage Books.

Shaywitz, S., & Shaywitz, B. (2008). Paying attention to reading: The neurobiology of reading dyslexia. *Development and Psychopathology, 20*(4), 1329–1349.

Shaywitz, et al. (2017). *Journal of Child and Adolescent Psychopharmacology: Developmental Psychopathology and Therapeutics, 27*(1), 20.

Silberman, S. *Neurotribes: The legacy of autism and the future of neurodiversity.* New York, NY: Penguin

Smith, D. D., & Tyler, N. C. (2014). *Introduction to contemporary special education: New horizons.* Upper Saddle River, NJ: Pearson Education.

Sorel, S. (2004). *Presenting Carly and Elliot: Exploring roles and relationships in a mother-son dyad in Nordoff-Robbins music therapy.* (Unpublished doctoral dissertation.) New York University, New York, NY.

———. (2010). Presenting Carly and Elliot: Exploring roles and relationships in a mother-son dyad in Nordoff-Robbins music therapy. *Qualitative Inquiries in Music Therapy, 5,* 173–238.

Sousa, D., & Tomlinson, C. (2018). *Differentiation and the brain: How neuroscience supports the learner-friendly classroom* (2nd ed.). Bloomington, IN: Solution Tree Press.

Spotkov, L. (2014). *Thoughts on using self-corrective instruction: An IBR activity.* Integrated ELA and Reading, EDU 506A. Molloy College, Rockville Centre, NY.

———. (2017a). *Ecosystems: Biomes around the world: An IBR activity.* Integrated ELA and Reading, EDU 506A. Molloy College, Rockville Centre, NY.

———. (2017b). *Ecosystems on stage: An IBR activity.* Integrated ELA and Reading, EDU 506A. Molloy College, Rockville Centre, NY.

———. (2018). *Ecosystem scavenger hunt: An IBR activity.* Integrated ELA and Reading, EDU 506A. Molloy College, Rockville Centre, NY.

Sullivan, A. (2018). *RTI and IEP: An explanatory narrative.* Stony Point, NY.

Suzuki, S. (1970). *Zen Mind, Beginner's Mind Quotes: Informal Talks on Zen Meditation and Practice.* New York: Weatherhill, Inc., 135.

Thompson, G., & McFerran, K. S. (2015). "We've got a special connection": Qualitative analysis of descriptions of change in the parent–child relationship by mothers of young children with ASD. *Nordic Journal of Music Therapy, 24*(1), 3–26.

Tobias, S., & Everson, H. T. (1995, April). *Development and validation of an objective measure of metacognition appropriate for group administration.* Paper presented at a symposium on "Issues in Metacognitive Research and Assessment," American Educational Research Association annual convention, San Francisco, CA.

Tomlinson, C. A. (1995). *How to differentiate instruction in a mixed ability classroom.* Alexandria, VA: ASCD.

Tomlinson, C. A., & Allan, S. (2000). *Leadership for differentiating schools and classrooms.* Alexandria, VA: ASCD.

Trinidad, J., & Liguori, M. (2016). *Know some states: Electroboard: An IBR activity.* Integrated ELA and Reading, EDU 506A. Molloy College, Rockville Centre, NY.

Valente, D., & LaCasse, K. (2018). *Moon phases find: An IBR activity.* Integrated ELA and Reading, EDU 506A. Molloy College, Rockville Centre, NY.

Warren, P., & Nugent, N. (2010). The music connections programmed: Parents' perceptions of their children's involvement in music therapy. *New Zealand Journal of Music Therapy, 8,* 8–33.

Webster's II New Riverside Dictionary (1996; Rev. Ed, Office Ed.). Boston, MA. Houghton Mifflin.

Whitman, K., & Amato, N. (2018). *Color mixing electroboard: An IBR activity.* Integrated ELA and Reading, EDU 506A. Molloy College, Rockville Centre, NY.

Wilcox, E. W. (1952). The way of the world. In *A treasury of the familiar.* Ralph L Woods (ed.). Cutchogue, NY: Buccaneer Books, 1.

Wills, A. (2017). *Number-line challenge.* Maple Road School 36, West Milford, NJ.

Yale Center for Dyslexia and Creativity. (2018). Retrieved from http://www.dyslexia.yale.edu/

About the Author

Reverend Dr. **Marjorie S. Schiering** has devoted her career as an educator to the concept of student-learners having a sense of self-efficacy, reliance, and empowerment. This is considered to be a direct result of the implementation and application of her experience-based Interactive Method (IM) of teaching and learning. Beginning in an inner city school in Columbus, Ohio, and then taking these ideas to North Carolina and upstate New York, she honed her concepts to include the teaching of thinking.

Dr. S., as she prefers to be professionally addressed, received her bachelor's degree in childhood education from the Ohio State University and earned her master's degree in reading from the College of New Rochelle, New York. Her doctoral work was done at St. John's University in instructional leadership. She wholeheartedly supports the concept of teaching students the way they best learn, along with their active involvement in the learning process.

Dr. S. has presented extensively and been published on the use of the IM with the Interactive Book Report book and workbook addressing critical and creative thinking. In 2003, she developed a Model for Academic and Social Cognition and had coauthors for a book that led to presentations on that model. She has also presented here and abroad on the topics of character development (*What's Right With You*, 2017), children's literature, and the ideas of one's being "enough" coinciding with her behavioral "No Put Downs . . . Only Lift Ups" philosophy. These presentations were primarily in the United States, England, Norway, Latvia, the Republic of Georgia, and South America.

Brain-based education, with emphasis on engaging one's imagination for the purpose of developing and enhancing one's creativity and critical thinking, have been two mainstays of her teaching endeavors. These have been accompanied by motivating teachers and students, inspiring learners to address their abilities, and creating a safe and positive classroom where there's a true sense of community.

Dr. S. is an ordained interfaith minister and served 10 years as a volunteer chaplain at Westchester Medical Center in Valhalla, New York. For the past five years she has been the advisor to Molloy's Circle K Club, which is a subsidiary of the International Kiwanis Club. She has presented at their state-wide NYSpeaking Conference many times. She continues to serve her community when called upon to do the promoting of positive thinking and human development for a sense of belonging where one lives and/or works. To that end, this past March she published her first children's book about mindfulness and keeping our environment safe.

www.ingramcontent.com/pod-product-compliance
Lightning Source LLC
Chambersburg PA
CBHW082213300426
44117CB00016B/2790